Causality
and
Determinism

Woodbridge Lectures
Delivered at Columbia University
in
October and November of 1972

Number Ten

Causality
and
Determinism

Georg Henrik von Wright

1974

Columbia University Press
New York   and   London

Library of Congress Cataloging in Publication Data

Wright, Georg Henrik von, 1916–
    Causality and determinism.

    (Woodbridge lectures delivered at Columbia University, no. 10, 1972)
    1. Causation.   2. Free will and determinism.
    I. Title.   II. Series: The Woodbridge lectures,
    Columbia University, no. 10, 1972.
    BD591.W74   122   74-11030
    ISBN 0-231-03758-9

Preface

These Woodbridge Lectures were given at Columbia on October 30 and 31 and November 1 and 2, 1972. I wish to thank the Department of Philosophy at Columbia University for honoring me with the invitation to give the lectures. They are published in a revised and slightly expanded form.

The present work has grown out of ideas embodied in the chapter on causation in my book *Explanation and Understanding*. Originally it was my plan to deal with the problems of causality and determinism both in the sphere of natural events and in that of human action. But I soon realized that it was not possible for me to discuss thoroughly both aspects of the topic within the set frame of four lectures. Therefore, the treatment is here restricted to causality as a category of a philosophy of nature only.

A first manuscript for the lectures was drafted during a stay at the Villa Serbelloni, Bellagio, in the Autumn of 1971. I am deeply grateful to the Rockefeller Foundation for this opportunity to do concentrated work in attractive surroundings. The first public presentation of the material took place in a series of Hägerström Lectures at Uppsala University in the Winter of 1972. My thanks are due to the university for inviting me and to my Swedish audience for the challenge to revise and improve the exposition of my thoughts.

Georg Henrik von Wright

Helsinki, Finland
November, 1973

Contents

Part I

1

2

3

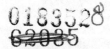

Contents

7

8

9

10

Contents

Contents

Part III

Contents

Contents

Part IV

1

2

3

Contents

Causality

and

Determinism

Part I

1

A few introductory words should be said about the aim and general character of these lectures.

I shall be talking here about *one* concept ("form," "type") of causation only—but one which I think is of sufficient importance to merit this singular attention. Its importance, as I see it, has many dimensions. First, this concept of causation is important because of the role it actually seems to play in scientific thinking and practice, particularly in the experimental and natural sciences. Secondly, it is important because of the even greater rôle it has played in philosophy as an ideal or model concept. It has set a model to philosophers of what a scientific "causal explanation" ideally looks like. And it has lent support to an idea according to which the entire course of the world, or of nature, is subject to a rigid determinism under inexorable causal laws.

One of my aims here is to show that this concept of causation is subject to certain inherent limitations. When these limitations are exposed, one can debunk as either illusory or trivial some of the exaggerated claims which philosophers traditionally have made for causation. My argument, to put it in a nutshell, will be this: The idea that causal connections are necessary connections in nature is rooted in the idea that there are agents who can interfere with the natural course of events. The concept of causation under investigation is therefore secondary to the concept of a human action. And this implies, as I shall try to show, that the idea of causal determinism, associated with this idea of causation, can claim validity only for limited portions of the world, and not for the world as totality. Thus causality and determinism are being put in their proper place, called to order, so to speak.

Nothing of what I am going to say, however, is intended to deny that one could talk meaningfully about determining factors (causes, determinants) and also about determinism in the realm of action. But the determinants of action, I would maintain, are of a totally different kind from causes and effects among events in nature. They fall under a different concept of causation and of determinism. Of this other form of determination, however, I shall not be speaking in these lectures at all.

An introductory remark should perhaps also be made about the "method" which I am going to use. This method consists largely in the application of tools of formal logic to an analysis of concepts of causation and determinism. It is only one method among many, and I do not claim that it is the best one even for achieving the philosophic aims which I here pursue. It may have limitations which restrict its philosophical applicability and significance. But it is the only approach to the problems which I can use myself with any hope of success or claim to novelty. And I think that, questions of ultimate philosophic success aside, this type of analysis is worth pursuing for the sake of the logical problems which it challenges and, in some cases at least, solves.

2

The causal relation and the notions of cause and effect can hardly be regarded as logical primitives. In the first instance one must try to "analyze" or even "define" them in the terms of some other notions. It is possible that these efforts will leave us with a residue of something "irreducibly causal." Still they must be made if the causal notions are to be assigned their proper place in a larger conceptual network.

There are several concepts, or groups of concepts, which might be considered plausible *explicantia* for causality.

One such concept is that of *function* (functional relationship). In a forceful and influential essay from the beginning of the century Bertrand Russell argued that, as a category of scientific thought, causality was becoming obsolete and was in the process of being replaced by notions of functional relationship. The lingering on of causal talk in the writings of philosophers was to be labelled a sort of atavism.[1]

Functional relationships of various types figure importantly in the formulations of laws, both in the natural and in the social sciences. Straightforward "causal laws"

[1] Bertrand Russell, "On the Notion of Cause," *Proceedings of the Aristotelian Society* 13, 1912–1913.

are perhaps not at all prominent in the more advanced theoretical disciplines. But what gives to some functional relations their nomic or lawlike character can, in my opinion, best be understood in terms of causal ideas. (See below III, 2.) For this and other reasons one cannot, as Russell seems to have thought, *dispense* with causality in favour of the concept of a function.

Another group of tools for analysing causality are various *probabilistic* and *stochastic* ideas. Probabilistic relations, for example between attributes of things or features of events, may be considered a special kind of functional relations. And, as in the case of functional correlations generally, the question of how to distinguish the accidental connections from the nomic ones is urgent also for probability relations. This differentiation may have to fall back on causal ideas. If this is the case, as I think it is, an account of causality solely in probabilistic terms cannot be adequate.

A third group of aids for explaining causality are, finally, the various concepts of *condition*. Whether causal relations can be exhaustively accounted for in the terms of conditionship relations is debatable. I think, however, that for a clarification of the basic conceptual features of causality, the analytic tools which condition concepts provide take priority over the concepts of function and of probability. The aid they provide will largely be relied upon here.

4

3

Logicians distinguish sufficient, necessary, and several other kinds of condition. It is usually thought that *one* condition concept, in combination with some logical constants and operators, suffices for the definition of all the other condition concepts. As basic notion can serve, *e.g.*, the concept of a sufficient condition.

The basic condition concept, whichever it be, is not a logical primitive, however. A Logic of Conditions must be built into some more "standard" logical theory. But which logical theory? Here two answers suggest themselves.

According to the one answer, the logic of conditions is a fragment of quantification theory. I shall call this the *extensionalist* view of conditions.

On the alternative view, condition theory is a fragment of modal logic. This will be called the *intensionalist* view of conditions.

Let p and q be two generic states of affairs. By calling states "generic" I mean that they can obtain or not, be instantiated or not, on different occasions (in space and time)—and thus obtain, and fail to obtain, repeatedly. An example of a generic state would be that the sun is shining. The sun may, at the same time, be shining in one locality but not in another or, in the same locality, be shining at one time but not at another; and the sun may be shining, and not shining, repeatedly.[2]

To say that the state p is a sufficient condition of the state q would, on the extensionalist view, mean some such thing as this: Whenever, *i.e.* on any occasion when, p obtains, q obtains too. (This is at best only an approximate explication.) The notion "whenever" is a temporal or tense-logical quantifier. We shall symbolize it by $\wedge$. If $\to$ is the sign for material implication, the universal implication $\wedge(p{\to}q)$ may be regarded as the groundform of a conditionship relation.

On the intensionalist view, to say that p is a sufficient condition of q can, for the purposes of a first approximation, be explicated as follows: Necessarily, *i.e.* it is necessarily the case that, if p obtains, then q obtains too. Let N symbolize necessity. On the intensionalist view, the groundform of a conditionship relation is a strict implication $N(p{\to}q)$.

The two views which we have distinguished should not be regarded as sharply exclusive of one another. First of all, there are combined uses of modal and quantificational notions. Secondly, it may be the case that a

[2] The *letters p, q, etc.* occurring in logical formulae are schematic representations of *sentences* describing (generic) states of affairs *e.g.*, of the sentences "the sun is shining" or "the ground is wet." When the letters occur in the text, either by themselves or in phrases such as "the state p" or "p obtains," they are schematic representations of the corresponding "that"—clauses, *e.g.*, "that the sun is shining" of "that the ground is wet." One could avoid this ambiguity by inserting the word "that" in the appropriate places and write, for example, "Let that p and that q be two generic states of affairs" instead of writing "Let p and q be two generic states of affairs." But this would be stylistically awkward.

fully developed theory of the quantifiers will have to employ modal concepts or that quantification theory, in the last resort, must be viewed as a fragment of modal logic. At least for the temporal quantifiers this possibility should be taken seriously. (See below I, 8.)

For the relation of sufficient conditionship between p and q we can also introduce the symbol $Sc(p,q)$ which is neutral as between an extensionalist and an intensionalist interpretation. For the relation of necessary condition we could have a symbol $Nc(p,q)$. This last, however, may also be introduced by definition, as follows:

$$Nc(p,q) =_{df} Sc(\sim p, \sim q).$$

That the obtaining of the state of affairs p is a necessary condition of, or is required for, the obtaining of q is tantamount to saying that the failing of the first to obtain is sufficient to guarantee the failing of the second.

4

It is a feasible proposal that every causal relation is a conditionship relation of some sort or other. But every conditionship relation is certainly not a causal relation. It can, for example, be a deductive, or otherwise "logical", relation between propositions. One will therefore have to single out *causal* conditionship relations from conditionship relations generally and distinguish them from *logical*, and possibly also from other, conditionship relations.

The following observation seems to show that this cannot be done, if one takes a purely extensionalist view of condition concepts:

When saying that p is a causally sufficient condition of q, we are not saying *only* that, as a matter of fact, whenever p obtains, q obtains too. We also claim that on all occasions in the past, when p did in fact *not* obtain, q *would have* obtained, *had* p obtained on those occasions. Only if the proposition that p is a sufficient condition of q warrants the truth of the counterfactual conditional proposition in question, does the conditionship relation here amount to a causal relation.

The counterfactual conditionals, which are thus entailed by, or can be "extracted" from, propositions to the effect that causal conditionship relations hold between "factors" (states, events, or whatever they be), I shall call *causal* counterfactuals. They are only one kind, among several, of counterfactual conditional propositions.

It is clear that a counterfactual conditional cannot be derived from the universal implication $\wedge(p \rightarrow q)$ in combination with the statement that its antecedent fails to obtain on some occasion. It is not off-hand clear whether it could be derived if we substitute for the universal the corresponding strict implication. But it is at least a plausible suggestion that an adequate account of causal conditionship relations ought, for the reasons

8

mentioned, to be given in "intensionalist", *i.e.* in modal, terms. For, what is it that warrants the "extractibility" of the counterfactuals from the causal relation, if not the fact that the bond by virtue of which this relation holds between p and q, in addition to being a universal, is also (somehow) a *necessary*, although *not* a *logically* necessary, connection?

A proposition which is necessary without being logically necessary I shall call *causally necessary*. Many philosophers doubt whether there are any such propositions—for example, because they think that there exists only one form of necessity, *viz.* logical necessity.[3] I consider this attitude too restrictive and think that in order to give a satisfactory account of causal conditionship relations one needs a notion of non-logical necessity. The question is, how to "make sense," so to speak, of such a notion. This question we shall discuss later, in Lecture II. In the rest of the present lecture I shall proceed as if the problem were already settled.

When a causally necessary and universal implication holds between two factors, p and q, there is what I propose to call a *nomic* connection or (causal) law connection between them. A nomic connection thus entails a corresponding universal implication, but is logically stronger than it. Not everything, however, which we call a Law of Nature is a causally necessary, universal proposition. (See below II, 6.)

---

[3] Cf. Wittgenstein, *Tractatus logico-philosophicus*, 6.37.

5

There are other observations which indicate that an analysis of causation in the terms of conditionship relations cannot be entirely adequate—independently of whether one takes an extensionalist or an intensionalist view of condition concepts.

Consider the symbol $Sc(p,q)$. Both if we interpret it as meaning the same as $\wedge(p{\rightarrow}q)$, or the same as $N(p{\rightarrow}q)$, we are forced to accept that it is logically equivalent with $Sc({\sim}q,{\sim}p)$. This means that the fact that a certain state obtains is a sufficient condition of the fact that a certain other state obtains if, and only if, the fact that the second state does *not* obtain is a sufficient condition of the fact that the first does *not* obtain.

Furthermore, $Sc({\sim}q,{\sim}p)$ is, by definition, equivalent with $Nc(q,p)$. Thus, by transitivity, $Sc(p,q)$ is also equivalent with $Nc(q,p)$.

Neither consequence need be thought objectionable for sufficient conditionship relations as such. But they become objectionable if we equate the sufficient condition itself with a cause, and that of which it is a sufficient condition with an effect of that cause. For example: heavy rainfall in the mountains might, under given circumstances, be a causally sufficient condition of a flood in the valley; but we are not inclined to say, at least not on that ground alone, that the fact that no flooding occurs is a *cause* of the effect that there is not

10

heavy rain. Similarly, it would be objectionable if the fact that rain is a *causally* sufficient condition of a flood by itself committed us to holding that the occurrence of a flood is a *causally* necessary condition of rainfall.

Take this second case first. Why is the consequence mentioned objectionable? A suggestion could be that a causal relation is not only a relation of conditionship between *generic factors* (states), but also requires a specific relation to hold between the *individual occasions*, in space and time, on which the states are instantiated. Is the requirement perhaps that the cause-factor(s) must be there antecedently in time to the effect-factor(s)? Or perhaps that, though cause and effect may co-exist in time, the cause must begin to exist before the effect? If we accept either answer, the causal relations between states would be conditionship relations between states on occasions which are, in some specific way, temporally related.

Whether this is the right way out of the difficulty, or not, this much seems certain: On one and the same occasion in time, or pair of successive occasions, only one of two generic factors, instantiated on the occasion or occasions in question, can "play the role of" cause relative to the other. The relation between cause and effect has an *asymmetry* or *directedness* which cannot be captured on the level of relations between generic states alone.

There is, as far as I can see, no logical absurdity involved in thinking that, on the generic level, the occurrence of a flood is a causally necessary condition of the occurrence of rain. For, might it not be the case that, unless a flood has occurred first, there will be no subsequent rainfall in the region—*e.g.* because the evaporation of the water of the flood is required for the formation of the rain-clouds? (I am, needless to say, not putting forward for consideration a meteorological hypothesis—it is the *logical* possibilities alone which interest us here.)

The difficulty connected with equating $Sc(p,q)$ and $Sc(\sim q,\sim p)$ is even more subtle. The pair of events *rain and a flood* and the pair *no flood and no rain* instantiate of necessity on different occasions, or successions of occasions. The asymmetry of the causal relation, if we think it is asymmetrical in the sense indicated above, is no obstacle to thinking both that rain causes a flood and that the absence of a flood causes the absence of rain. Nor is there, as far as I can see, any other logical obstacle to thinking this. The oddity is solely that it cannot be a *logical consequence* of the fact that rain causes a flood that the absence (or ceasing) of a flood would *cause* rain not to occur (or to stop pouring). Both causal relations are possible here, but they are (logically) independent of one another. An analysis of causation in the terms of conditionship relations will not, by itself, show that this is so. Therefore this analysis cannot capture all the logical features of the causal relation either.

6

The basic ontological categories used in the present investigation are those of a generic state of affairs and of an occasion.

States are atomic (elementary) or molecular (complex, compound). Arbitrary states will be referred to using schematic letters $p, q, \ldots$ or sequences $p_1, \ldots, p_n, \ldots$ and their compounds will be referred to using compounds formed of such letters and the connectives $\sim$, $\&$, $\vee$, $\rightarrow$, and $\leftrightarrow$, for negation, conjunction, disjunction, (material) implication, and (material) equivalence respectively. It is assumed, without argument, that such compounds can be handled according to the rules of ("classical", two-valued) propositional logic (PL).

A generic state of affairs obtains or does not obtain on a given occasion (in space and time). The coupling of a generic state with an occasion can be said to constitute an *individual* state of affairs.

The notions of state and occasion are loaded with problems. These problems we shall here ignore. "One has to begin somewhere."

It may be thought that the *static* category of a state is unsuitable as a basis for a logico-philosophical theory of causality and that its place should be taken by a *dynamic* category. One such category is that of a *process*, another that of an *event*.

13

It may be suggested, moreover, that the category of process is primary in relation to the category of state. This challenge to our treatment here of causality may be said to be implicit in Hegelian logic. It will not, however, be taken up for consideration.

The category of event, on the other hand, seems to be secondary to the category of state. For an event can be regarded as a change, or transformation (in time), among states. For example: the state p obtains on some occasion but $\sim p$ on a subsequent one. Then the event of p's passing away or vanishing or becoming destroyed has taken place. Conversely, if the obtaining of $\sim p$ is succeeded by p, then p has come to be or happened or occurred. These are events. "By logical courtesy," one may also regard as events the staying on of a state or its continued absence. (See also below III, 3.)

As I shall try to show later, causal relations are primarily relations between events and not between states. But if I am right in thinking that events may be accounted for in the terms of states and temporal relations between occasions, states retain their place as belonging in a basic ontological category in our account of causality.

Consider a set $p_1, \ldots, p_n, \ldots$ of logically independent states. That the states are logically independent shall mean that, on any given occasion, they may obtain or not in any one of the logically possible combinations. (The meaning of "may" here is that of *logical* possibility.) If the number of states in the set is n, the number of such combinations is 2^n. Any one of the combinations corresponds to a different compound state. These compound states will be called possible *total states* of a world or, for short, *possible worlds*.[4]

This notion of a world is relative to a given set of states. It is a fragment or an aspect of "the real world", characterized or described in the terms of the states of the set.

According to a certain philosophical view, there exists a set of logically independent states such that a complete description of the real world, at any given stage in its development, can be given by telling in which total state, composed of the members of this set, the world is at that stage. This view will here be called *logical atomism*.

It is part of the logico-atomistic world view that the total states of the world are not only composed of logically independent elementary states but also logically independent *of one another*. This logical independence of the total states themselves means that any given total state, whenever it obtains, *may*, as far as logic goes, be succeeded by the same or by any other total state. There are, one could also say, no *logical* dependencies *in time*. What is true at any one time is logically independent of what is true at any other time. This may indeed be regarded as one of the most fundamental, and also most

[4] The term "possible world" should be used with caution. What is "possible" here is not "the world" but that the world, at a certain stage of its development, should be in a certain total state. The world is not the total state. The world, one could say, is *that which* is now in one, now in another, total state.

problematic, tenets of logical atomism. (That it is not so often mentioned and discussed is probably due to the fact that discussions of logical atomism have mainly been concerned only with an assumedly static world, ignoring the aspects of world development.

The history of the world is a temporal succession of total world states. On the generic level this means a succession of events. On the individual level the various moments in this succession are occasions in time. Can these occasions be counted, as they occur, or is their density that of the rational or even that of the real numbers? The alternatives mentioned answer to a conception of the time-medium as discrete or compact or continuous respectively.

On the assumption that time is discrete and the total number of elementary states is finite and equal to n, the total number of possible histories of the world over a succession of m occasions is 2^{mn}. It can be said that m measures the *length* of this history and n the *width* of the world.

The question may be raised whether the width of the world is fixed, or whether it may wax and wane in the course of the history of the world. The answer will depend upon what one thinks are the "building-bricks" or constituents of states of affairs. One plausible suggestion is that these constituents are individual things, properties, and relations. A discussion of these ontological categories, particularly of the notion of an individual thing, may be important to a full understanding of cau-

16

sality. But, as already indicated, these aspects of the ontology of causation will not be touched upon here.

In the following discussions we shall employ an extremely simple logico-atomistic model or picture of the world. This model assumes that the number of elementary states is *constant* and *finite* and that time is a *discrete* flow of successive occasions.

I do not maintain that this model is true of the real world. But I shall maintain that the real world in some of its aspects or to some degree exhibits the logico-atomistic structure of the model. (Cf. below III, 5.) It is also my view that the features of the world which are mirrored in this model are essentially connected with a concept of causation of prime importance both to scientific thinking and to philosophic speculation about the world order.

7

Consider an arbitrary occasion in time, a "now" separating the past from the future. On this occasion the world is in a certain one of the (logically) possible total states. Let a circle represent this total state. As far as logic is concerned, the world may on the next occasion be in any one of the 2^n total states which can be composed of the n logically independent elementary states which, we assume, provide the "building bricks" of our world. On the freedom of the world's development there may, however, exist restrictions. I shall refer to them as *causal* restrictions. Let k be the number of total states in which the world, as far as causality is concerned, may be in on the next occasion. We can illustrate these k possible developments by k circles in a vertical row to the (immediate) right of the circle representing the total state which obtains now and connected with it by lines. Any given one of these k circles can be connected with circles in a vertical row to *its* (immediate) right. These latter circles then represent the total states which would be possible on the next occasion, should the total state represented by the given circle come to be the total state of the world on the occasion next after now. Thus we generate a tree picturing the possible future histories of the world:

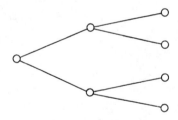

The different total states are not individuated in the picture. Two circles can represent the same or different total states. By convention, any two circles which are connected with the *same* circle to their immediate left shall represent *different* total states of the world.

The number k may vary within the limits from 1 to 2^n

inclusive. The fraction $\dfrac{k-1}{2^n-1}$ can be used as a measure of the *degree of determination* (or of freedom) of the (immediate) development of the world at any given stage of its possible history. For $k=1$, this degree is 0. Then the course of history is rigidly determined from a hypothetical "now" to the next moment. For $k=2^n$, this degree is 1. Then there is complete non-determination ("indeterminism").

8

Consider again an arbitrary "now" and the corresponding total state of the world. I shall refer to this couple of an occasion and a total state as "the world today." That an elementary state p obtains (in the world) today means that it is a conjunctive part of the total state in question.[5] When this is the case, we shall also say that the statement that p obtains is *true of* the world at that stage, *i.e.* today.

The next occasion after the arbitrarily selected "now" I shall call "tomorrow." What does it mean to say that an elementary state p obtains (in the world) tomorrow?

It cannot mean that p is a conjunctive part of at least one of the total states which are possible for tomorrow.

[5] That the state p is a conjunctive part of a total state means here that the (schematic) sentence "p" is a conjunct in the corresponding (schematic) state-description.

For this answers to the statement that p will *perhaps* obtain tomorrow. I shall denote this statement by "$\vec{M}p$".

Thus the statement $\vec{M}p$ is true today if, and only if, p is a conjunctive part of at least one of the total states which are causally possible for tomorrow. When $\vec{M}p$ is true of the world at a certain stage, we shall say that p itself is a *potency* or *latent possibility* of the world at that stage. As far as causal restrictions are concerned, the world at that stage may (immediately) develop into a world in which p obtains.

Assume that p is a conjunctive part of every one of the total states which are causally possible for tomorrow. Then it is true of the world today that p will *certainly* obtain tomorrow. This statement I shall denote by "$\vec{N}p$". It is easily seen that $\vec{N}p$ is equivalent with $\sim\vec{M}\sim p$, *i.e.* is the negation of the statement that the world today has a potency of (immediately) developing into a world of which it is *not* true that p obtains in it then.

If it is a certainty about the world today that p will obtain tomorrow, then p will be there tomorrow *no matter what else happens to the world, i.e.* independent of whatever other features in the world will change or remain unchanged from today to tomorrow.

When I assert "it will be raining tomorrow," what do I assert? Am I saying that it will perhaps be raining tomorrow, that this, in the light of facts and laws of meteorology, is a possibility—or even is highly probable? No, for then we should say so. Maybe we thus modify our assertion, if pressed by questions such as "Are you sure?" or "How do you know?" But if we are not willing thus to modify our assertion, then what we maintain is that certainly, no matter what else happens to the world, it will be raining tomorrow.

The statement that it will certainly be raining tomorrow can be understood in at least two senses, however. (And the same is true of the statement that it will perhaps be raining.) It can be taken in an *ontic* sense, meaning that the facts which are true of the world, together with the laws ("laws of nature") regulating the development of the world, *determine* tomorrow's weather in such a way that *it* is certain to be raining tomorrow. Or it can be understood in an *epistemic* sense, meaning that "for all we know" it will be raining, the facts and laws as known to us indicate that it will be raining, *we* are certain that it will be raining tomorrow.

A supporter of determinism would say that, ontically, it is certain that it will be raining or certain that it will not be raining tomorrow. Ontically, in the world (in nature), there are no causal alternatives. Ontically, the picture of how the world develops from a given "now" towards the future, is not that of a branching tree but that of a linear succession of total states. Epistemically, because man is not omniscient, *our* picture of how the world develops has to count with alternatives and therefore have the form of a tree.

Determinism, in a nut-shell, is a philosophic position which denies the existence of *real*, *i.e.* causal, alternatives in nature. (See below IV, 4.)

The view which I am taking here is not committed to determinism, but admits the possible existence of *causal* (real) alternatives in nature. The future, on this view, is *open* or, topologically speaking, is a branching tree of alternative world-developments. Whether, and in what sense, this view is *compatible* with determinism is another question, to which I shall return in the last lecture.

The formal logic of the concept $\vec{M}$ I shall refer to under the name "the logic of tomorrow". It is the logic of the potentialities of immediate change inherent in a world at an arbitrarily selected stage (a "today" or "now") of its development. One could also call it the logic of the words "certainly" and "perhaps" when applied to that which is immediately ahead of us.

It is easy to see that this "logic of tomorrow" is a weakened form of the system of modal logic often called the System *M*. The weakening consists in the fact that the *ab esse ad posse* principle, $p \to \vec{M}p$, fails to hold. From the fact that a state *p* obtains today it does not follow that it will perhaps obtain tomorrow as well.

Another principle which fails to hold in this logic is $\vec{M}\vec{M}p \to \vec{M}p$. Here the antecedent says that it is a potency of today's world to become "overnight" a world with a potency of becoming "overnight" a world in which *p* obtains. $\vec{M}\vec{M}p$, in other words, signifies a potency of a world of becoming a *p*-world the day after tomorrow. And from this, of course, it does not follow that the world may become a *p*-world already tomorrow.

We next introduce a new symbol $\vec{\nabla}$. $\vec{\nabla}p$ shall mean that the state *p* will perhaps obtain, *i.e.* it is causally possible that it obtains, in the world at *some* future stage. $\sim\vec{\vee}\sim p$ then says that it is not the case that p may fail to obtain in the world at any future stage. As an abbreviation for this statement we shall also use the symbol $\vec{\wedge}p$.

Speaking in the terms of our topological illustration, that $\vec{\vee}p$ holds true in an arbitrarily selected "world today" means that at some stage in some of the possible histories of the world which may evolve from the world today the state p will obtain.

The formal logic of the concept $\vec{\vee}$ (and $\vec{\wedge}$) I shall refer to as "the logic of the future."

The iterated form $\vec{\vee}\vec{\vee}p$ holds true of an arbitrary "now," *i.e.* holds true of the world at an arbitrary stage of its development if, and only if, it holds true of the world at some stage in some possible development after the "now" that p will obtain at some stage in some possible development after *it*. But then it is also the case that p obtains at some stage in some possible development after the "now." Thus, for the logic of the future, the principle $\vec{\vee}\vec{\vee}p \rightarrow \vec{\vee}p$ (and the dual principle $\vec{\wedge}p \rightarrow \vec{\wedge}\vec{\wedge}p$) is valid.

It is easy to see that the logic of the future is a weakened form of the system of modal logic known as S4. The weakening consists in the fact that the *ab esse ad posse* principle fails to hold. From the fact that p obtains at some stage of the world's development it does not follow that p may obtain again at some later stage.

We now turn our view towards the past, counting

from an arbitrarily selected "now." The immediately preceding stage in the world's development I shall refer to as "yesterday".

To say that p obtained yesterday is to say that p is a conjunctive component of the total state which immediately preceded the present total state of the world. There is but *one* such total state, and immediately before it there was another one, and so forth in a linear succession towards an ever remoter past. We may not *know*, whether p was there yesterday or not—but, *no matter what has happened since, p was or p was not*. The past, unlike the future, is *ontically closed*. The history of the world, when looked at in the direction towards the past has no alternative courses "behind" itself. At each stage in the past it may have had alternative courses "ahead of" itself. But these alternatives were "consumed", step by step, as the world evolved.

I shall introduce the symbol $\overleftrightarrow{M}p$ for the statement that p obtained yesterday. ($\overleftrightarrow{M}\overleftrightarrow{M}p$ then says that it was true of the world yesterday that p obtained yesterday, *i.e.* it says that p obtained the day before yesterday.)

The logic of $\overleftrightarrow{M}$ I shall refer to as "the logic of yesterday". It too is a modal logic. It is, moreover, a modal logic of a particularly simple structure in which the difference between the necessary and the possible is obliterated. For, to say that p obtained yesterday, $\overleftrightarrow{M}p$, obviously is equivalent with saying that it is not the case that p did not obtain yesterday, $\sim\overleftrightarrow{M}\sim p$. This "collapsing" of the distinction between the possible and the necessary does not make the system uninteresting as a modal logic. Quite to the contrary. Speaking in the traditional modal terms, one can call it a modal logic of a universe of propositions which has no room for contingent propositions but in which every truth is a necessity and every falsehood an impossibility.

This modal system has no received name. I shall call it the System R.

Next we introduce a symbol $\overset{\leftarrow}{\nabla}$. $\overset{\leftarrow}{\nabla}p$ shall mean that the state p has come to obtain in the world either now or at some stage already past. $\sim\overset{\leftarrow}{\nabla}\sim p$ accordingly means that this state has up to and including the present stage in the world's history never failed to obtain. For this we have the abbreviation $\overset{\leftarrow}{\wedge}p$.

The logic of the symbol $\overset{\leftarrow}{\nabla}$ (and $\overset{\leftarrow}{\wedge}$) we can call "the logic of the past" or of that which has come to be, when the past is counted up to and including the present.

A characteristic law of this logic is expressed by the formula $\overset{\leftarrow}{\nabla}p\,\&\,\overset{\leftarrow}{\nabla}q \;\leftrightarrow\; \overset{\leftarrow}{\nabla}(p\,\&\,q) \;\vee\; \overset{\leftarrow}{\nabla}(p\,\&\,\overset{\leftarrow}{\nabla}q) \;\vee\; \overset{\leftarrow}{\nabla}(q\,\&\,\overset{\leftarrow}{\nabla}p)$. It says that two states, p and q, have come to obtain in the world if, and only if, they have obtained on one and the same occasion, *i.e.* simultaneously, or one of them, p or q, has obtained after the other. In this principle is embodied the *linear*, and in this sense causally closed, structure of the past.

The logic of the symbol $\overset{\leftarrow}{\nabla}$ (and $\overset{\leftarrow}{\wedge}$) is structurally identical with the system of modal logic called S4.3.[6]

---

[6] On the equivalence between systems of modal logic and of tense-logic see also the Appendix.

9

We can make a combined use of our tense-logical concepts and symbols for speaking about *all* time whether past, present, or future.

The formula $\overset{\leftarrow}{\vee}p \vee \overset{\rightarrow}{\vee}p$ says that the state p either has already obtained at some stage in the world's history or will perhaps obtain later. As an abbreviation for this statement we shall use $\vee p$.

Analogously, the formula $\overset{\leftarrow}{\wedge}p$ & $\overset{\rightarrow}{\wedge}p$ says that the state p has up to now always obtained and will certainly continue to obtain in future ("no matter what else happens to the world"). This will be abbreviated $\wedge p$. (Cf. above I, 3.)

Just as the world now has an open future of unactualized possibilities, the same was the case with every past occasion. As the world evolved from the past, parts of this future became closed. Thus is might happen that a state p which once was a potency of the world, but which did not materialize, may no longer come to obtain. One can then speak of it as a "lost possibility." That p is a lost possibility is expressed in symbols as follows: $\overset{\leftarrow}{\wedge}{\sim}p \& \overset{\rightarrow}{\wedge}{\sim}p \& \overset{\leftarrow}{\vee}\overset{\rightarrow}{\vee}p$. To be read: "$p$ is not, never was, and never will be, but there was a time in the past, when p might have come to be at some future time."

Some state may be such that, not only has it always as a matter of fact obtained, but it was also always certain that this state was going to obtain in all future. That p is such a state is expressed by the formula $\overleftarrow{\wedge}p\&\overleftarrow{\wedge}\overrightarrow{\wedge}p$. As an abbreviation for this expression we shall use $\wedge p$.

If $\wedge\ p$ holds true, then the state p will be called a *causally necessary* state. If $\wedge p$ holds true, we shall say that p is a *universal* (universally obtaining) state.

It is readily seen from the definitions, and the logical laws governing the symbol $\overleftarrow{\wedge}$, that $\wedge p$ entails $\wedge p$. A causally necessary state also universally obtains, but not *vice versa*. If $\wedge p$ holds, but not $\wedge p$, we shall say that p is *accidentally universal*.

10

Are there causally necessary states, *i.e.* states of affairs which of causal necessity obtain at every stage in the world's history? That is: is a statement of the form $\wedge p$ ever true?

The answer probably depends partly upon what is meant by a "state of affairs." It may be thought that elementary states cannot be, in themselves, causally necessary. But which states then shall count as "elementary" ?

Independently of these controversial questions, however, it seems obvious that molecular (compound) states may be necessary—more specifically states which are disjunctions of other states. Consider, for example, the compound state $\sim p\vee q$, or, which is the same, $p\rightarrow q$. That this state is causally necessary means that, at every stage in the world's history, necessarily either the state p does not obtain or the state q obtains. In other words: necessarily, if p obtains, then q obtains too.

This type of statement may be regarded as a prototype form of a nomic connection. (Cf. above I, 4.) It entails the weaker statement which says that, as a matter of fact, at every stage in the world's history, either the state p does not obtain or the state q obtains. (Above I, 9.)

Accordingly, the symbolic expressions $\wedge(p \rightarrow q)$ and $\wedge(p \rightarrow q)$ are prototype forms of statements of nomic necessity and universal regularity respectively. But they represent, at best, only first approximations.

It may be thought that the states which are connected by a nomic tie must themselves be causally contingent. One could express this same condition by saying that the antecedent state p must not be causally impossible, nor the consequent state causally necessary. The symbolic expression for the law would then be $\vee p \& \vee \sim q \& \wedge(p \rightarrow q)$. This entails $\vee \sim p$ and $\vee q$. The conjunctions $\vee p \& \vee \sim p$ and $\vee q \& \vee \sim q$ mean that p and q are causally contingent.

Some doubts may be voiced whether two states in *the same* total state of the world can be nomically connected. "Is simultaneous causation possible?" But whether the answer is affirmative or negative it seems certain that a nomic connection often (one is inclined to say normally or typically) is between temporally related states. And then the question will arise: *how* related temporally?

28

In a discrete time-medium two relations seem of particular importance. One is when the nomically related factors (states) are supposed to materialize on two immediately successive occasions in time. We shall call this the case of *contiguity*. The other is when there is a "time-gap" separating the materialization of the factors. Then we may speak of causal "action at a distance."

The question whether causally (nomically) related factors may be temporally separated without there existing a contiguous causal "chain" joining them is another big problem in the philosophy of causality.

The statement which says that, necessarily, if the state p obtains or obtained at any stage in the world's history, then q certainly obtains or obtained at the next stage, can be expressed in symbols as follows: $\wedge(p \rightarrow \vec{N}q)$. Assuming that the world has no beginning in time, this is equivalent with saying that, necessarily, if p obtained at any stage immediately preceding a given one, then q obtains at that given stage. In symbols: $\wedge(\tilde{M}p \rightarrow q)$.

$\wedge(p \rightarrow \vec{V}q)$ is the prototype form of a statement to the effect that two factors, p and q, are connected nomically but their materialization is perhaps separated by a time-interval of indefinite length.

I shall assume that, if two factors (states) are connected by a causally necessary and universal implication of the prototype form $\wedge(\rightarrow)$, possibly with some contingency and related clauses added to it, then one can, on any instantiation of the two factors under the law, single out at most one of them as cause-factor relative to the other which is then effect-factor.

If the cause-factor is a causally sufficient condition of the effect-factor, we call the first simply *cause* and the second simply *effect* on that occasion of their instantiation. But if the first is a causally necessary condition of the second, it is neither common nor natural to speak of them as simply "cause" and "effect." Calling them cause- and effect-*factors* respectively sems, however, unobjectionable.

If it were established that "the cause must precede the effect," then it would follow from the proposition $\wedge(p \to \vec{N}q)$ that p is, on any instantiation, cause and q effect. $\wedge(q \to \overleftarrow{M}p)$ says that p is a causally necessary condition of, and thus a cause-factor in relation to, q. The second statement can also be written $\wedge(\sim\overleftarrow{M}p \to \sim q)$ which is equivalent with $\wedge(\overleftarrow{M}\sim p \to \sim q)$ which in its turn is equivalent with $\wedge(\sim p \to \vec{N}\sim q)$. The last formula says that $\sim p$ is a causally sufficient condition and thus a cause of $\sim q$. As noted earlier (I, 3), statements about causally necessary conditions can be translated into statements about causally sufficient conditions and thus about causes.

If, however, we have to account for simultaneous, or even for retroactive, causation, the situation is more complicated. Then the structure of the nomic connection $\wedge(\ \to\ )$ does not by itself decide which of two connected factors is "cause" and which one "effect." The cause-effect distinction then depends on the nature of each occasion when the two factors instantiate. The distinction may yield different results on different occasions. Thus, for example, it is not possible from the form $\wedge(p \rightarrow q)$ to tell whether p is a causally sufficient condition of q, or q a causally necessary condition of p. The causal relation between the two factors may on some occasion be the one, on other occasions the other. Problems connected with the cause-effect distinction in the case of simultaneity will be discussed later (II, 1).

Generally speaking, if two causally contingent factors are connected by a causally necessary universal implication, then the two factors are causally related. But which of them is cause and which one effect may vary with the occasions on which the factors instantiate.

11

It may be regarded as a defining feature of a *nomic* generalization that it allows counterfactual conditionals to be extracted from itself for cases in the past. (See above I, 4.) In order to check that this actually is the case with the formulations $\wedge(p{\rightarrow}q)$ and $\wedge(p{\rightarrow}\vec{N}q)$ for such generalizations, but not with the weaker formulations $\wedge(p{\rightarrow}q)$ and $\wedge(p{\rightarrow}\vec{N}q)$, we must first look for a way of expressing counterfactual conditionals in the symbolic language which is now at our disposal.

What do we say when we say that *had* p been the case, on some occasion, q *would have* been the case too, on that occasion—or on the next one? In the statement is contained, I think, four things. The first is that p *is not* the case on the occasion in question. In symbols: $\sim p$. The second is that it *was* certain that, either p was not going to be the case on that occasion, *or q* was going to be the case on that occasion—or on the immediately succeeding one. In our symbolism: $\overleftarrow{M}\overrightarrow{N}(\sim p \vee q)$ or $\overleftarrow{M}\overrightarrow{N}(\sim p \vee \overrightarrow{N}q)$. The third thing is the statement that it was not certain that p was *not* going to obtain, *i.e.* $\overleftarrow{M}\overrightarrow{M}p$. The fourth, finally, is that it was not certain either that q *was* going to obtain or to follow immediately, *i.e.* $\overleftarrow{M}\overrightarrow{M}\sim q$ or $\overleftarrow{M}\overrightarrow{M}\overrightarrow{M}\sim q$. If the third and fourth clauses were not satisfied, the counterfactual conditional statement would be trivialized. The full expression of the counterfactual is thus

$$\sim p \& \overleftarrow{M}\overrightarrow{N}(\sim p \vee q) \& \overleftarrow{M}\overrightarrow{M}p \& \overleftarrow{M}\overrightarrow{M}\sim q$$

or, alternatively,

$$\sim p \& \overleftarrow{M}\overrightarrow{N}(\sim p \vee \overrightarrow{N}q) \& \overleftarrow{M}\overrightarrow{M}p \& \overleftarrow{M}\overrightarrow{M}\overrightarrow{M}\sim q$$

depending upon whether q is supposed to materialize simultaneously with p or immediately after.

The statement that had p been the case, q would have been the case too, I shall call a *categorical* counterfactual conditional statement. It is clear that such statements are not entailed by the nomic generalizations under discussion. For the generalizations do not entail that there have been, or will be, occasions when p did, or will, in fact not obtain. The "extraction" of counterfactual conditional statements is only for *hypothetical* cases of p's failing to obtain—and it is for *all* such cases, both those *already* past and those *not yet* past. This generalized hypothetical counterfactual has the form

$$\vec{\wedge}\overleftarrow{\wedge}[\sim p\,\&\overleftarrow{M}\overrightarrow{M}p\,\&\overleftarrow{M}\overrightarrow{M}\sim q\rightarrow\overleftarrow{M}\overrightarrow{N}(\sim p\vee q)]$$

when p and q are simultaneous. And it has the form

$$\vec{\wedge}\overleftarrow{\wedge}[\sim p\,\&\overleftarrow{M}\overrightarrow{M}p\,\&\overleftarrow{M}\overrightarrow{M}\overrightarrow{M}\sim q\rightarrow\overleftarrow{M}\overrightarrow{N}(\sim p\vee\vec{N}q)]$$

when q is supposed to succeed p immediately.

The first generalized counterfactual statement will be true if $\wedge(p\rightarrow q)$ is true—and the second will be true if $\wedge(p\rightarrow\vec{N}q)$ is true. For, the first nomic generalization guarantees that at no stage in any possible history does the total state of the world contain as a component the conjunctive state $p\,\&\sim q$. And the second guarantees that there is no possible succession of states $\sim q\,\&\overleftarrow{M}p$. The universal implications $\wedge(p\rightarrow q)$ and $\wedge(p\rightarrow\vec{N}q)$ give no such guarantees. The non-nomic generalizations are compatible with the possible existence of states $p\,\&\sim q$ or successions $\sim q\,\&\overleftarrow{M}p$ which never actualize.

12

The logic of time (or perhaps we should rather say of world-development) as here sketched, is thus a complex of four different structures. These are the S4-like logic of the open future, the M-like logic of the successive steps towards the future, the logic R of the successive steps back in time, and the logic S4.3 of the closed, linear past.

A schematic picture of the development of the world, over 5 successive stages, could look like this:

33

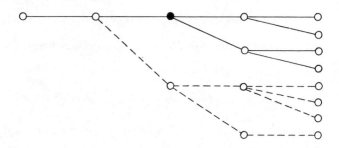

The black circle represents the present total state of the world. The histories along the dotted lines picture developments which once were, but no longer are, possible for the world. They thus represent "lost possibilities."

The openness of the future is here conceived of as an *ontic* openness. Ontically, the future is open (branching) and the past closed (linear). Past and future are thus, in a characteristic sense, *asymmetrical*.

One could argue against the asymmetry between the past and the future in two ways:

One way is to argue that both directions of time are, in fact, branching. This would be uncontroversially true in the *epistemic* sense. For, epistemically, both past and future are open. Just as we do not (always) know for certain what is going to happen, do we not (always) know for certain what was the case—but have to allow for a bundle of alternative (past) possibilities. A topological picture of such an epistemic world-perspective, viewed from a given present state, could be the following:

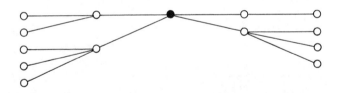

One could, however, also argue that both directions in time are linear. This is the position of determinism. The indeterminism, the openness of the future, would have to be labelled an "epistemic illusion." The alternative world-developments reflect our ignorance of how the world will develop. This is a well-known position from the history of thought.

A convinced determinist would say that my world-picture consists of an ontic past and an epistemic future—hence the appearance of "asymmetry". On the ontic level there is symmetry, *viz.* linearity in both directions—and so also on the epistemic level, *viz.* openness in both directions. This is not how I would see it. But the question is complex and crucial and we shall have to say something more about it later on (IV, 10).

Part II

1

In the first lecture we distinguished between accidental regularities and nomic connections in the concomitance and succession of states of affairs.

Let it be the case that the state q obtains on every occasion when p obtains. Then there is a regularity of concomitance of p and q. This regularity is *nomic* if its holding good is a matter of (non-logical) necessity. It is *accidental* if its holding good is *only* a matter of fact, not a matter of necessity. But what does this distinction amount to, between "mere fact" and "necessity"?

The distinction, I think, refers in the first place to instances in the past. On some occasions in the past p obtained, on others not. Let us assume that on all occasions when p obtained, q was there too. If this was a necessity, and then only, are we entitled to say, in retrospect, that *had* p obtained also on those occasions in the past when in fact it did *not* obtain, then q too would have been there. If we are not entitled to maintain this, the regularity was accidental only.

The reference to the past, however, is not to the past from any particular present, but applies to all "future pasts" as well as to anything "already past." If therefore the concomitance of q with p is nomic, then on any (now) future occasion of which it *will be* true to say that *p did not* obtain then, will it also be true to say that, had *p* obtained then, *q* would have obtained too.

The difference between "fact" and "necessity," which we are anxious to pin down, is thus attributable to the inherence in the latter, but not in the former, of an element of "counterfactual conditionality." (Cf. above I, 4 and I, 11.) The counterfactual conditionals that are derivable from nomic universal implications in conjunction with singular statements to the effect that their antecedents fail to obtain we called (I, 4) *causal* counterfactual conditionals.

As is well known, a universal generalization, though in principle falsifiable through the occurrence of a single counterinstance, can never be strictly verified. This is so, independently of whether the truth of the generalization is accidental or nomic. But this fact does not yet settle the question whether there are some observations or tests for deciding (verifying, making plausible) whether a generalization which has so far held true in experience is accidental *or* nomic.

Metaphorically speaking, what is required for this decision is a dive under the surface of actual reality into the depths of unactualized possibilities, the "lost possibilities" of an ever growing past. Of cases when *p* was *not* there we should have to show that, *had p* been there, *q would have* followed. Clearly, this is not possible for all the potentially infinitely many cases when *p* is missing. But is it possible even for a single case?

Can a singular counterfactual conditional statement ever be verified? In order to verify it, we should have to substitute for a state which obtained at a certain stage in the world's history another state which did not obtain at that very stage. In any straightforward sense of "verification" this is certainly not possible. The past is "closed," a *fait accompli,* and we cannot do anything to open it up again.

Thus, if a counterfactual conditional statement can be verified at all, it can be this only in some *oblique* sense. Which could this oblique sense be?

Not all counterfactuals are causal. The answer to the question of "verification" might be different for the different types of counterfactual. Here we are concerned only with the "verification" of such counterfactual conditionals that are thought to be derivable from causal laws.

In practice, such counterfactuals are often made plausible by reference to the very laws themselves. The water in the kettle would have boiled if heated to a certain temperature. The statement partakes in the certainty of a "law of nature." But how do we know that the familiar uniformity has not been accidental only? What has made us sure that it supports counterfactuals?

The question is: Which are the independent criteria of lawlikeness, the ascertained presence of which would constitute an oblique verification of counterfactuals? As I see it, to ask for criteria of (causal) lawlikeness and to ask for a verification procedure for (causal) counterfactuals is to ask for the same. And the answer, I think, must be sought along the following lines:

The past is closed, but the future, we said, is open.

38

This implies that, although we cannot interfere with the past and make it different from what it *was*, we may be able to interfere with the future and make it different from what it otherwise *would be*. It is on this possibility, *viz.* of interfering with the "normal" course of nature, that the possibility of distinguishing the nomic from the accidental ultimately rests. The clue to an understanding of the epistemic problem here thus lies in the logical peculiarities of the concept of an action. These we must now examine in some detail.

2

What is it to act? Maybe the category of action is too comprehensive or too vague to permit an illuminating answer to the question as a whole. But for a great many important cases the following answer seems a good one:

To act is to interfere with the course of the world, thereby making true something which would not otherwise (*i.e.* had it not been for this interference) come to be true of the world at that stage of its history.

To say that an action has taken place, for example that a man has been murdered, is to say, explicitly, that, thanks to an agent, something has come true of the world, *viz.* that a man is now dead, and to contrast this, implicitly, with something which would otherwise have been the case, *viz.* that this man is still alive. The object of this implicit reference I shall call *the counterfactual element* involved in action.

If that which comes true through an action is contradictorily opposed to something which was true immediately before, we call the action *productive* of that which came true or, alternatively, *destructive* of that which was true. If again that which comes true, as compared with what would otherwise have been the case, is the same as that which was true immediately before, we call the action *preventive* of that which would otherwise have come true or, alternatively, *sustaining* of that which already was true. Opening a door which would otherwise remain closed is productive action; keeping a door open which would otherwise close is preventive action.

If no agent interferes with the world at a certain stage of its development, something comes true which would not have come true had somebody acted. This fact is of special interest when an agent's failure to interfere has the character of intentionally abstaining or forbearing from an action which he could have performed. Depending upon whether the omitted action would have been productive or preventive, we then say that he (intentionally) *leaves* something unchanged which would otherwise have changed or that he *lets* something change which would otherwise have remained unchanged.

The thing, the coming true of which is a logically necessary condition of a certain action having been performed, I shall call the *result* of this action. It may stand in a causal relation of some sort to some other things which are also true of the world. These other things can be referred to as either (causal) *consequences* or (causal) *prerequisites* of the (performance of the) action in question.

It is on purpose that I speak vaguely of that which comes true through action as "something" or as a "thing." Under the atomistic conception of the world, which we entertain here, that which comes true through action is some state of affairs. The change which consists in the coming into being of this state from the contradictory state is an *event*. For the sake of terminological convenience, we may also call the non-change which consists in the remaining (continuing) of the same state an event. (Cf. III, 3.)

In the concept of an action is thus implicit a comparison or contrast between a state of affairs resulting from the action and another state which would otherwise, *i.e.* had it not been for the performance of the action, have obtained. But of that which "would otherwise have obtained" we cannot possess "strict knowledge," if it is thought that such knowledge is possible only of that which we witness (observe, verify) as having occurred. For that which "would otherwise have obtained" never comes true (occurs). It is "contrary to fact."

Even though we, in a sense, cannot "strictly know" the counterfactual to be true, we may have a firm conviction that it is true (be confident in or certain of its truth). On this implicit trust in counterfactuals rests our conviction that we perform actions and that we are agents who *can act*.

Consider the following elementary illustration to this:

On the desk in front of me there is now a loose sheet of paper. I know I can turn it over if I want to. Implicit in this knowledge of my ability is my confidence that the paper in front of me will remain in its present position, unless I turn it. Should I exercise my ability and turn the sheet, I could afterwards say confidently that, had I not interfered, the sheet would have remained in its present position. It happens, of course, that I am mistaken. Perhaps a sudden breeze through the room turns the paper in front of me the very moment when I am about to do it myself. But this is exceptional. If such cases were common, they would weaken my confidence in my *ability* to perform the action. And if it was the rule that sheets of paper turned over and whirled about quite unpredictably most of the time, there would be no such *action* as turning over a sheet of paper.

The notions of an action and of ability to act thus presuppose confidence in and familiarity with a certain amount of regularity in the course of events in the world. This confidence we sometimes vest in counterfactual conditional statements to the effect that such and such would have been the case had we not interfered with the world.

If there did not exist a certain amount of regularity, there would not be confidence in and familiarity with it either and, *a fortiori*, we should not have our present notions of agency, action, and ability. Action can thus be said to presuppose regularities in the world. This does not mean, however, that action presupposes causality and the existence of nomic connections in nature.

Here it is important to observe the difference between those counterfactual conditionals which are presupposed in action and those which are involved in nomic connections. The latter we have called *causal* counterfactuals. The counterfactuals presupposed by actions are *not* causal. When, for example, I say that the sheet of paper in front of me would have remained in its previous position had I not turned it over, I do not intimate that there was a cause keeping it in that position which was then "counteracted" by my interference. What I intimate is rather that there was no (other) cause which would have turned the sheet over when *I* did it. The confidence which I here have in the truth of a counterfactual conditional is a confidence in the *absence* of causes which would disrupt the continuation of a state of affairs which I have come to regard as *normal.* The confidence which I have that the water in the kettle would have boiled if heated is a confidence in the difference which the presence of a cause would have made to the prevailing situation. According to the view for which I am trying to argue, confidence of the latter kind presupposes confidence of the former kind. That is: confidence in the effects of causes (nomic connections) presupposes confidence in the causeless continuation of certain normal states of affairs. (But we shall presently see that the relation between these "layers of confidence" is complex—and that there is an asymmetry in the way productive and preventive actions are related to the absence and presence of causes. See III, 4–5.)

3

Assume that we have witnessed several times in the past that, without exception, the state p has been followed immediately by q. Assume further—on the ground of these observations or for some other reason—we think that it always was and will be so. But we are not yet sure whether the connection is nomic. Is it also true of the great many cases when p was not there that, had it been there, q would have followed?

Suppose that p is a state which we can produce when it is not there. This implies, according to what was said in the preceding section, that there are situations in which p is not there and of which we feel confident that p will continue to be absent, at least for some short time, unless we interfere. We feel confident, moreover, that we *can* change these situations so that p will be there.

On an occasion of this kind we now make the following "experiment": We change the situation to one when p obtains and observe what happens with regard to q. Suppose we find that q, which had been absent too, is there ("dives up") on the next occasion. This will "impress" us—unless we had some independent reasons for thinking that q would have come to be there in any case.

This experiment we next supplement with the following observation: In a new situation, of a similar generic character, when p is absent, we refrain from interfering and let p continue absent and watch what happens with regard to q. Suppose we find that q, which had been absent, continues to be absent. This will confirm that we were justified in being "impressed" by the result of our previous experiment.

If the supplementing observation is close in time to the experiment and if the circumstances surrounding the two situations seem moderately stable, *i.e.* do not seem to us to have changed in relevant respects, then, in what has taken place we have come as "near" as is *logically* possible to the verification of the counterfactual conditional statement which says that, had p been there on the occasion when we let it remain absent, q would have followed.

It seems that our confidence in causal counterfactual conditionals and in the nomic concatenation of things have their root in the kind of complementary experiences which we have just described: doing something and noticing that a certain thing follows; refraining from doing and noticing that the same thing does not follow.

By contrast, our confidence in the non-causal counterfactuals presupposed in action is of a more "primitive" kind. It is a component of our knowledge of our *ability* to do certain things—for example, produce the state of affairs p. This confidence can, if challenged, easily be put to empirical test. We refrain from producing p in a situation when p is not there but could, we think, be produced by us—and notice that p continues absent then. On the whole, such tests are successful. Sometimes they fail. If they often fail, we begin to doubt our ability to produce p "ourselves." If they were to fail normally, we should not claim to have the ability at all. (Cf. above II, 2.)

The question may be raised: *Why* is it that the experiment and the supplementing observation described above should have the effects on our beliefs which they actually seem to have? Is there anything in the *logic* of the situation which can explain or motivate this?

There are at least two possible cases when the sequence of q upon p might be regular (universal) *without* being nomic.

One is, when there is a *common cause* of both p and q, *i.e.* some third state r which is a causally sufficient condition of the appearance of p and then q. If this is the case, we do not say that p causes q. Nor are we then prepared to assert, for any occasion when p is *not* there, that, had p been there, q would have followed. For example: If we press the burning tip of a cigarette against a sheet of paper, there will first appear a brown spot on the paper and then, in the same place, a hole in the paper. We do not say that it is the appearance of a brown spot on the paper which causes the hole to appear. Nor do we say that, had a brown spot appeared on a paper where in fact it did not appear, then a hole too would have appeared. We might, however, be prepared to assert the counterfactual in question if we do not know, or suspect, any *other* (generic) cause of brown spots on paper (than contact with some burning hot object) which also produces a hole. Provided namely that

46

we also feel convinced that every appearance of a brown spot on a sheet of paper must be caused by something, *i.e.* cannot appear causelessly. (A deterministic conviction.)

This possibility of a common cause of p and q is eliminated by the experimental interference and subsequent observation of q. For the fact that p is produced by us presupposes that, had we not produced it, p would not have come to be—and thus it excludes the existence of a common cause of p and q here. That is: as long as we stick to the statement that *we* produced p, we cannot acknowledge such a cause. To do this would be to withdraw the statement that we acted.

A second case, when the sequence of q upon p might be regular without being nomic, is the following: In the situations noted by us when p is absent, q will come about "in any case", *i.e.* independently of whether we produce p or not. If this were so, we should describe the result of our experimental interference by saying that *even though* p was there q followed, *i.e.* we should think of p as something the presence or absence of which does not hinder the cause of q, whatever this may be, from operating. We ought, therefore, to perform the active experiment in a situation when we think that otherwise, *i.e.* were it not for the experiment, q will not appear. It is this assumption which we "verify" by refraining from the interference and passively watching what then happens.

None of these operations exclude the possibility that q may have other sufficient causes besides p. But in

47

order to show that any factor, p or some other, bears this relationship to q, we must be able to *disentangle* it from other factors with the same relationship to q, study it in a situation when it *alone* operates. It is for this reason that we require that, when we refrain from producing p, we shall not witness q either—unless in some exceptional cases when another cause of q happens to operate. But these cases must remain exceptions, and not be the rule. If they were common, the causal role of p in relation to q would remain obscure.

4

I am arguing for the existence of intrinsic connections between the concepts of cause and nomic necessity on the one hand and the concepts of action and agency on the other hand. I try to argue, moreover, that the first concepts presuppose, are dependent upon, the second ones.

There is a time-honored idea that agency is itself a form of causation—in fact its basic or primary form. Agency is sometimes called *immanent* causation and causal connections "in nature" are called *transeunt*. It has been suggested that the idea of transeunt causation was in origin a "projection" of the to us familiar relation between agent and nature onto relations between natural events or states. Causes operating *in* nature were conceived of on the pattern of agents operating *on* nature.

48

The talk about agency as cause can be understood in a way which is, if not identical with, at least closely related to the position for which I am arguing here. But I greatly prefer, for the sake of clarity, a different way of speaking about things.

I am anxious to *separate* agency from causation. Causal relations exist between natural events, not between agents and events. When by *doing p* we *bring about q*, it is the *happening* of p which *causes q* to come. And p has this effect quite independently of whether it happens as a result of action or not. The *causal* relation is between p and q. The relation between the agent and the cause is different. The agent is not "cause of the cause," but the cause p is the *result* of the agent's action. The effect q is a *consequence* of the action. (See above II, 2.) The relation between the result and the action is intrinsic. The result must be there, if we are to say correctly that the action has been performed.

The existence of specific causal relations, and the operation of causal factors, is thus independent of agency and of the interference of agents with nature. One could express this by saying that causation is *ontically* independent of agency. So, how then shall we characterize the dependence which we claim that there is of the first (causation) on the second (agency)?

The question which led us to assume this dependence, it should be remembered, was the question how to distinguish between nomic and accidental regularities. The distinguishing feature, we suggested, was that nomic generalizations provide a valid basis for making counterfactual conditional assertions.

The question how to come to know whether a regularity satisfies this criterion of lawlikeness is an *epistemic* question. It will readily be admitted, I think, that for the purpose of answering this question experiments are crucial. It is, in the last resort, by subjecting generalizations to the kind of "systematized observations" we call experiments that we test and establish their nomic, as distinct from accidental, character. Is this all there is to the claim that causation is dependent on action? Shall we say that the dependence of the first on the second is only *epistemic?*

To answer these questions affirmatively would, however, be to misunderstand the nature of the claim. The dependence of causation upon action is *conceptual.* The dependence, moreover, is not directly one between cause and action, but between the notion of a (causal) counterfactual conditional and action. And since there is an apparently indisputable conceptual relation between causal connection and counterfactual conditionality, it follows by transitivity that there is also a conceptual relation between causal connection and action.

The notion of a counterfactual conditional is the notion that something would have been different from what it actually was, if——. As said before: There simply is no way of verifying whether a counterfactual conditional statement is ever true. But there is a characteristic "substitute" for a verification. A man has learnt to do various things. In learning this he has acquired *a* notion of counterfactual conditionality, *viz.* the one inherent in the notion of an ability. An ability to do things is a "power" to interfere with "nature" to make the course of the world (a little bit) different from what it otherwise would be. If now we observe a regular sequence between two states in the world, and if one of the two is a state we can produce, then we may, by producing it, succeed in bringing about the other as well. (The criterion of success is, then, not only that the other state comes about, but also that on similar occasions, when we do *not* exercize our ability, the other state usually remains absent.) If this turns out to be the case, we vest the first of the two states with a "power" of producing the second state, *analogous* to our power of producing the first. We then say that the first state is a *cause* of the second. But what this comes to, over and above a statement of regular sequence, is that, if we *could* produce (could have produced) the first state on an occasion when it does (did) not obtain, we should bring (have brought) about the second in consequence. This statement can be made also about states the production of which is not within our ability—and the statement is true or false quite independently of whether we or anybody else ever acquire the ability.

But could one not object to this, saying: What the causal statement amounts to, over and above regular sequence, is merely that if the first of the two states had obtained on an occasion when in fact it did not obtain then the second state too would have come about. In this formulation there is no talk about action at all. *If p* causes q, then if I can produce p, I can also bring about q. The statement about action possibilities *follows* from the causal statement. So, am I not in fact trying to reverse the logical order here? Could it not be the case, for example, that we have observed a regular sequence of q upon p, time after time, and then come to think that p causes q without ever contemplating the production of p? I am not denying that this is possible. But as long as we cannot, or do not, interfere with the situation, the possibility remains that it is *not* the case that p causes q, but *is* the case either that there is a third factor, say r, which causes the joint successive appearance of both p and q or that the regularity is accidental. These rival hypotheses about the nature of the case would remain possibilities as long as we do not subject the regularity to experimental test. Until we can produce p—if not quite generally so at least under laboratory conditions—we cannot perform this test. When we are sure we *can* produce p, but not until then, we can make sure that p *may* have the power of producing q. And only then can we make plausible that it actually *has* this power, by using our ability to produce p for bringing about q under conditions when we are also confident (on the basis of observations) that q will not occur independently.

If man throughout stood quite "passive" against nature, *i.e.* if he did not possess the notion that *he* can do things, make a difference to the world, then there would be no way of distinguishing the accidental regularity from the causal one. Nor would there be any way of distinguishing the case when p has the "power" of producing q from the case when some factor r has the "power" of producing the sequence of q upon p. Man would simply not be familiar with the notion of counterfactuality, with the idea of *how it would have been, if———. This* is the ground for saying that the *concept* of causal connection rests on the *concept* of action.

Thus the suggested "objection" turns out not to be any objection at all. It is true that, in addition to affirming a regularity, the causal nomic statement only says that, had the first of two states obtained when in fact it did not, then the second of them would on those occasions have obtained too. But in making this addition we employ a notion, *viz.* that of the counterfactual conditional which we should not have if we did not also have the notions of action and agency.

It may be illuminating to compare the position for which I am arguing with that of Hume. A major part of Hume's efforts were devoted to the problem of how we come to associate the idea of necessity with observed regular sequences. This is the problem which engages us too. Hume gave his answer in psychological terms. The observation of regular sequence engenders an association of ideas. With the associative tie a mental "conditioned reflex" is established so that henceforth the observation of the cause alone calls forth the idea of the effect.

Hume's answer to his question was ingenious, and criticism of it has not always been fair. Yet I think it will not do as a solution to the problem. My proposed way out is different. The idea of necessity, which we associate with some regularities, arises from observations we make when we interfere and abstain from interfering with nature. The fact that the observations have this effect on us reflects conceptual peculiarities of the notion of acting (interfering with nature). The idea of action is an idea of how to make a difference to the world, and from this idea of a potential difference is born the idea of a necessary connection. If we were not familiar with action and ability to act, we should not have the further notion, in a sense opposed to it, of "iron laws of nature." For we should then have no means of distinguishing between accidental and lawlike uniformities.

One could say that, both on Hume's view and on the view taken here, causal necessity is not to be found "*in nature.*" In nature there are only regular sequences. But it would also be wrong to say that causal necessity exists only "in our minds," that it is something "subjective" and not "objective." Action requires an agent, an acting subject. To this extent the concept of an action, and also that of causal necessity, is "subjective." But that there are agents and actions and lawlike connections is not in any reasonable sense of the term to be labeled "subjective." It is, on the contrary, something which in its turn has an "objective" foundation in facts of nature, as I shall next try to show.

5

A man is born into a society with characteristic institutions and traditions. The education to which he is subject belongs to the institutionalized traditions of the society. In this surrounding he acquires the concepts which he has. The concepts thus have a foundation in the historical and social setting of the culture to which a man belongs.

But concepts also have another foundation, *viz.* in facts of the world. We can imagine the world differently constituted from what it is and imagine that the differences would affect our concept formation. Imagining this will again have to take place within a given conceptual framework. It is an illusion, of which philosophers too often are victim, that we are free to imagine anything which is not contrary to the laws of logic. But, within limits, imagining a different world is possible— and sometimes constitutes a philosophically useful move.

Thus it is, I think, legitimate to ask which requirements the *facts* (the world) must satisfy in order that there shall exist a *concept,* roughly at least like ours, of nomic causation. To the answer the following seems relevant:

First, the world must to some degree approximate to the model of logical atomism. It must be possible for us to recognize in it conceptually and verificationally separable instantiations of generic states of affairs. The states, moreover, must be such that the verification of the fact that one of them obtains or does not obtain on a given occasion does not by itself settle the question whether another one of them obtains or not on that same occasion. This is a requirement of logical independence. (Cf. above I, 6.)

There must also be situations which are sufficiently

like one another to make it feasible to speak of the *repeated* occurrence of some of their generic features. With some (many) such situations we must, moreover, be able to *interfere*. This implies a conviction about what *would* happen, or not happen, if we do not interfere. It implies, in other words, a conviction about a "natural" course of events which is independent of our interference. (Cf. above II, 2.)

Furthermore, there must exist regular successions between phenomena. This regularity must not be confused with the repeatability required by the ideas of action and interference. Action presupposes that certain features of situations will continue or not, depending upon whether we interfere or not. But causation presupposes, in addition, that the features of the world which are thus dependent upon us will, when they appear in the world, be with a fair amount of regularity succeeded by other features.

Finally, a certain amount of discreteness seems to be required in the temporal succession of states (events). It must be possible to separate *occasions* in time and characterize them by the states which obtain or do not obtain on these occasions. In a world of perpetual change and flux this would not be possible—and such a world would provide no "foothold" either for our notion of action or for that of causation, at least not in their present form.

It would be bad metaphysics to say that "really" there are no conceptually and verificationally separable states in the world, no discrete occasions, no repetition. (Yet this has been said—also by good metaphysicians.) But it would be equally bad metaphysics to assert that reality has the logico-atomistic structure of our world-model. (This too, or something very much like it, has been maintained.) This structure, and alternatives to it, are *models* to which "the world" may approximate to some degree. And some "fragments" or "regions" of the world may approximate better than others. The degree of approximation is reflected in the concepts which we have and consider useful to employ. In a region of the world where approximation is low, concepts connected with the model become accordingly less applicable. This holds true also for the concept of causation which we are here trying to clarify.

Because of its relation to action, this concept of causation might be termed *actionist* or *manipulative* causation. Considering its close connection in scientific contexts with the mode of action called experiment, *experimentalist* causation would be another appropriate name for it.

6

I have argued that the possession and application of the concept of experimentalist causation imposes certain requirements on the build of the world. Next, we must briefly consider to which extent the world meets these requirements. The solution to this problem again partly depends upon what is included in the *concept* of "the world."

Is, for example, agency part of the world, or not? One

sometimes makes a division of the world into "man" and "nature." How the line of division has to be drawn is difficult to tell. Man as a living body is obviously a part of nature too. But man as agent may have a different status. One also makes a corresponding distinction between the natural and the human sciences. But here too the line of division is wavering and its significance debatable. Those philosophers who put strong emphasis on the unity of science also tend to take a monistic view of the logical structure of the world.

Independently of our stand on the metaphysical questions, it will readily be admitted, I think, that the idea of experimentalist or manipulative causation has obvious and important applications in the natural sciences—and also that its applicability becomes debatable when we move to the human (including the social) sciences. If we wish to identify causation as such with manipulative causation, we could then say that the category of causation is primarily at home in the (experimental) natural sciences and basically alien to the human sciences. If again we do not wish to make this identification, we may instead distinguish *types* of causation and say that causation in the natural sciences is primarily of the manipulative type, whereas in the human sciences another type (or other types) of causation and of causal explanation are prominent.

Accepting these rough statements about the limits of (types of) causation, one can raise further questions: Is causation in the experimental natural sciences *always* of the manipulative type? Has the category of manipulative causation any application *at all* to the human and social sciences?

The second question I shall not discuss in these lectures. The answer to the first question is, I suggest, "essentially affirmative." The following considerations will be offered in support of this suggestion:

Observed regularities in nature, which have not or cannot be put to experimental test, we do not unhesitatingly or unquestioningly regard as "causal" or "nomic." We might classify them with Mill under the heading "empirical laws." [1] It sometimes happens that such uniformities are subsequently raised to the rank of "causal laws." This seldom, if ever, takes place as a consequence of continued confirmation alone. Something "has to be done" to the law. Sometimes what happens is that we succeed in "explaining" it. This normally means that we succeed in deducing it from some other laws which already have an unquestioned nomic character, or in showing that the new law is but a special case of an established one.[2] But how did the laws from which these deductions were made get their nomic character? An answer to this question is that *they* have been accessible to experimental test under normal laboratory conditions.

Regularities of nature are often observed in regions which are out of reach of human interference in space or

[1] *A System of Logic.* Bk. III, Ch. xvi.

[2] *Ibid.,* § 1: "To state the explanation, the *why*, of the empirical law, would be to state the laws from which it is derived; the ultimate causes on which it is contingent."

in time. Astrophysics, cosmology, and geology deal largely with such "remote" parts of the world. Why do we think that the *same* laws of nature which govern phenomena in the to us familiar spatio-temporal surroundings should be valid in those remote parts of the universe too? Whence the *semper et ubique* which we associate with the idea of the reign of law? These are intriguing questions. I think that an important aspect of the answer to them is that we do not acknowledge as "laws" empirical regularities which cannot be related, deductively or otherwise, to the bulk of laws over which we have experimental control in our laboratories.

Not all accepted laws of nature, however, are themselves inductive generalizations or experimentally tested nomic connections. A great many among the most important ones of them have a conceptual, rather than experiential, character. Such laws or principles are sometimes said to be *true by convention*. They are neither confirmed nor refuted by the testimony of experience. They serve rather as standards for interpreting the findings of experiments and observations. The law of inertia or of conservation of energy are perhaps of this character. The "discovery" of both of them was intimately connected with experimental research; the acquisition of the notion of inertia can indeed be said to have been the laying of one of the cornerstones of the early fabric of experimental physics. But neither of them is a causal law or else an inductive generalization.

There is no hard and fast classification of laws of nature into conceptual and experiential. A principle which, in some contexts, for some purposes, is treated as open to test is, in another context, for some other purposes, "frozen" into a conceptual standard.

A contrast is sometimes made between causal or deterministic laws of nature and stochastic or probabilistic ones. Some writers think that causal laws are at bottom only high degree statistical correlations—others think that probabilistic laws presuppose underlying causal uniformities. I think both views are wrong. The fact that one sometimes lays aside exceptions to causal laws rather than lets the laws be falsified does not show that the laws are "really" only high degree correlations. (Cf. below III, 5.) Probabilistic laws of nature do not rest on causality, but the influence of factors on the probability of events can often be described as "causal." This is so particularly when the factors can be manipulated and the effect of their presence or absence tested in mass-experiments. The "probabilifying effects of causes" is a classic chapter of inductive logic awaiting fresh treatment. I shall not attempt to deal with it here. Suffice it to say that the importance of probability in natural science does not infringe upon or detract from the importance of causality or nomic connections.

Part III

1

After our discussion, in Lecture II, of the relation between causation and action, we are ripe to attack a problem which was raised in the first lecture. I called it the problem of the *asymmetry* of the causal relation. (Cf. above I, 5.) The asymmetry, roughly speaking, consists in this: If *p* causes *q*, then *q* does not cause *p*. But, as was already pointed out (I, 5), this asymmetry does not reside in the relation of the *generic* factors, *p* and *q*, considered by themselves. It resides in their relation on individual occasions of their instantiation or occurrence. *When, i.e.* on an occasion when, *p* causes *q*, it is not the case that *q* causes *p*. But on some other occasion their roles may be reversed. The problem now is: What determines, in the individual case, which factor is the cause and which one the effect?

It was also (I, 5) hinted at the following possible answer to the problem: Cause and effect should instantiate on successive occasions in time. What comes first is the cause and what comes after is the effect—provided that the factors are nomically connected. But this answer, by itself, cannot be satisfactory. For, by accepting it we should have excluded, at the very outset and without further argument, the possibility of simultaneous causation. And, problematic as the notion of simultaneous causation may be, we cannot reject it just because of the simultaneity of the occurrence of the two related factors.

In Lecture II an idea was introduced which may help us handle the present problem. It is a characteristic of a causal relationship, we said, that by manipulating the cause we should be able to control or regulate the effect.

This way of distinguishing cause from effect seems, in normal cases, to coincide in its result with the first way, which bases the cause-effect distinction on temporal precedence. For, what our actions bring about or call forth normally follows *after* the interference. But the distinction on the basis of interference, unlike the distinction based on temporal order, refers to individual pairs of instantiations of the causally related factors. Moreover, it provides a means of making this distinction also in cases when there is no order of temporal precedence to be distinguished at all. This means that accounting for the cause-effect asymmetry in terms of action and interference caters, at least in some cases, also for the possibility, excluded by the temporality view, that cause and effect may occur simultaneously.

Consider the following imagined case: There is a container with two valves, a top one and a bottom one. The state of affairs when the top one is open I shall denote by "$\sim p$", and the state when the bottom one is closed by "q". Imagine that the valves are so connected that, when the top valve closes, the bottom valve opens, and *vice versa*. Further imagine that the two changes take place absolutely simultaneously. (I think this experiment of thought encounters no logical difficulties—but the question may be worth a fuller discussion than we give to it here.) We witness these changes a number of times. We become curious to know whether they are causally connected and, if so, which is cause and which is effect here.

The mere fact that there is some kind of "connecting mechanism" between the valves does not settle the question. We must also know what makes it operative. Only then can we judge its causal relevance to the changes in the positions of the valves.

Assume now that *we* can operate the two valves ourselves, *e.g.* that we can shut the top one by pressing it with our hand and that we can open the bottom one by pulling. We do the first and see the bottom valve open. We do the second and see the top valve close. Under normal circumstances we should feel convinced that the changes are causally connected. Moreover, we should think that, on the first of the two occasions, it was the closing of the top valve which caused the bottom valve to open and that, on the second occasion, it was the opening of the bottom valve which caused the top valve to close. The two changes occur, for all we can see, simultaneously. And yet we confidently distinguish them as cause and effect.

Now the question may be raised: Is it only when the situation originates through active interference with the states of the valves that we can distinguish between cause and effect here?

Suppose the situation is $\sim p\&q$ and that a stone falls

down from the sky and hits the lid of the top valve so that the valve closes and the bottom valve opens. We do not know from where the stone came or whether it was dropped by somebody. Obviously the hitting of the upper valve by the stone acted as cause here. But how shall we describe its causal role? Did the hit of the stone close the top valve and the closing of the top valve open the bottom valve? Or did the stone cause both the closing of the top and the opening of the bottom valve? Or was it perhaps so, that what the stone did directly was to open the bottom valve (to "knock it open") and that it was the opening of the bottom valve which caused the top valve to close (by "pulling it down")?

We should, of course, dismiss the third possibility at once. But why? Obviously, because we know from past experience and analogous situations that lids of a certain construction and in an open position shut when we apply to them such pressure as, among other things, a falling stone can effect. We have seen this happen in cases when there *was* no bottom lid to be opened at all, *etc.* We have learnt to apply such pressure ourselves— with our hands directly, or with a hammer indirectly, and perhaps with dropping stones too. If doubted whether a stone can have this effect on the valves, we can make an experiment.

It would be more difficult to exclude the second alternative, *viz.* that the stone both closed the top valve and "knocked open" the bottom valve. In fact, it is quite possible that the hit of the stone had these *two* effects. If an inspection of the container would not reveal any-

65

thing which we should recognize as a "mechanism" connecting the valves, we should hardly think of the states of the valves as causally connected mutually, but think of them as causally related to a common cause. Similar observations apply to the case, when *we* close the upper valve by pressing the lid.

(Be it noted in passing that to recognize a connecting mechanism is possible only for one, who is already familiar with analogous cases or who takes the trouble to experiment with the supposed connection.)

Assume, however, that we have satisfied ourselves that the stone did not open the bottom valve directly but that the latter opened as an effect of the closing of the top valve. How could we know that the *top* valve did not close for some quite different reason, or quite accidentally for no reason at all, and that the stone did not just "passively" follow the movement of the lid? In the last resort, I suggest, we know this on the basis of experiments and of our confidence in certain non-causal regularities. The valves must be such that they do not often change their positions, seemingly for no reason; we can rely that they will continue in their present positions, unless certain things happen to them; and we can ascertain that the hit of a stone is a thing of this sort by dropping a stone on the lid in a situation when we feel confident that it will not close "of itself."

What makes it possible to *distinguish* cause from effect in the case under discussion is thus either that we can produce the one state and thereby bring about the other *or* that we can identify a cause of the coming

66

about of the one state which is not also (directly) a cause of the other. In order to establish that the "cause of the cause" (for example the fall of the stone onto the lid) is not directly a cause also of the "effect of the effect" (for example the opening of the bottom valve) we must be familiar with situations in which there is not an opportunity for the original cause-effect sequence to occur. (We must, for example, experiment with containers which have only one lid to shut and to open.)

Cause and effect in the example under discussion are distinct, if *there is* a cause of one of the two simultaneous changes, even though there may be no observer to distinguish the cause from the effect here.

But what if, at the same time as a cause of one of the simultaneous changes operates, the other change takes place either thanks to (direct) interference or thanks to the operation of some (direct) cause? For example: At the same time as a stone hits the lid of the upper valve, closing it, some force from below pulls open the bottom valve. If this were to happen, and it *can* happen, we should not think of the two simultaneous changes as causally connected on that occasion at all—but attribute the occurrence of each of them to a separate cause (or view them as the results of two different actions).

Assume, however, that the two states originate simultaneously but that there is no "cause of the cause" for either of them. Nor do they come about as the result of interference. This is possible—unless we introduce a deterministic principle to the effect that nothing can come about without either being produced by action or caused by something. To think that such a principle *must* hold true would be sheer "deterministic dogmatism," however. The case which we are now imagining is surely a (logical) possibility. If this possibility were to materialize, we should not have to deny that the two changes are causally connected. But there would then be nothing to distinguish the cause from the effect. We need not say that, on such an occasion, the two states cause *one another* to be. At least there is nothing which would compel us to say this. We *may* say that their simultaneous origination is, in this case, a mere coincidence. But if otherwise we have reason to think that there is a causal connection between them, it would be unnatural and unnecessary to make this exception. The best thing to do is to admit that two simultaneously originating states may be *causally connected*, even though the *cause-effect distinction* (separation) is *not always* applicable to cases when the states originate.

2

A great many laws in the natural sciences have the character of functional relationships between measurable factors. Consider such well-known elementary examples of laws in physics as the Gas Law, or Snell's Law, or Ohm's Law. In its most simplified form the gas law says that, at unvarying temperature, the product of the volume of a gas and the (external) pressure to which it is subject is a constant. $v \cdot p = c$.

One would not ordinarily speak of this as a "causal law." But it would be quite in order to say that the factors v and p are "causally related." To a variation (change) in the one there will answer a definite variation (change) in the other. Moreover, by varying the pressure we can vary the volume. We know of no reciprocal way of varying the pressure by varying the volume. Hence we think that, when there is a co-variation in the two factors, it is always the variation in pressure which is cause and the variation in volume which is effect.

It is characteristic that the causal relation here is most naturally conceived of as a relation between changes (histories) and not between states. This is perhaps so, because p and v themselves do not represent *specific* states. They stand for variables or determinables, the values or determinates of which represent specific states (of pressure or volume). And there seems nothing unnatural about saying that, in a secondary sense, a specific state of pressure causes a specific state of volume.

When, in the above example, the situation is such that the determinate which is the cause always belongs to the same determinable, and similarly the determinate which is the effect, then one can also distinguish the variables (determinables) as independent, *i.e.* causing, and dependent, *i.e.* caused. (This is a familiar distinction.)

It is perhaps right to say that the more advanced a branch of exact science is, the more prominent is the role played in it by laws which have the character of functional (mathematical) relations between determinates (values) of determinables (variables). Such laws, as we have seen, are not ordinarily spoken of as causal. The advance of science towards types of law which are, in the sense explained, not causal may have contributed to the view expressed by some philosophers that causation has become progressively obsolete and unimportant in science. (Cf. above I, 2.) But this is to misunderstand the situation. The basis of functional laws are causal relations between (variations in) determinate states. The way in which these relations are established is normally highly typical of the way in which we acquire true causal knowledge, *viz.* through experimental interference with nature.

3

Let us go back once again to the example of the two valves. If the state of affairs is that the upper valve is closed (*p*) and the lower valve open ($\sim q$), we could not tell whether the first is closed because the second is open, nor whether the second is open because the first is closed—not even assuming that the two states are causally connected. In order to tell which is cause and which is effect, we must dig into the history of the case, try to get to know how the present state of affairs came to be. This observation indicates that the causal laws at operation in this and other cases are, primarily, not laws connecting *states of affairs* but laws connecting *events*.

I think this must be accepted as an important truth

about causation—or at least about that concept of causation which we are here trying to clarify. This notion is essentially a *dynamic* notion, relating to changes in nature. I have so far, mainly but not quite consistently, been talking of causes and effects as states and of causal laws as state-relating principles. For purposes of a first approximation and for reasons of simplicity this may be permissible. But the time has now come when we must replace the simplified manner of speaking by a more accurate and fuller one.

First some words should be said about the concept of an event.

An event, generally, may be defined as a change or transformation among states of affairs. But in order to make this definition work, something ought to be said both about the (relation between the) generic characters of the states in question and about the (relation between the spatio-temporal) occasions on which the states instantiate.

One can define an *elementary event* as the changing of a (generic) state of affairs into its contradictory or opposite, *e.g.* from p to $\sim p$, on a pair of occasions which are adjacent either spatially or temporally or both. We shall not here go into the question whether the adjacency of the occasions presupposes that space and time are discrete media. We may, for our purposes, disregard the complications inherent in the notion of an occasion.

The change from the generic contradictory of a state to the state itself, *e.g.* from $\sim p$ to p, is of course also an

71

elementary event. The first change is the event of coming to be, the second that of passing away.

What is the negation of an event? This idea is not clear by itself and can be defined in more than one way. Here I shall by the negation of the event of p's coming understand the absence of p on both of two (adjacent) occasions; and by the negation of the event of p's passing away the presence of p on two successive occasions. The negation of an event, under this conception, is thus a not-change or *constancy* with respect to a state of affairs.

When speaking of causal relations between events, we must also pay attention to the negations of events, the constancies. That this is necessary is very clearly seen when we consider the interrelatedness of causally sufficient and causally necessary conditions. If a change from $\sim p$ to p is sufficient to produce a change from $\sim q$ to q, then, by definition (cf. above I, 3), the continued absence of p is necessary to warrant the continued absence of q, and *vice versa*.

Considering that both changes and constancies, *i.e.* events and their negations, may be terms in causal relations, we can distinguish the following four possibilities for relations of sufficient conditionship: 1. A change is a sufficient condition of another change. 2. A change is a sufficient condition of a constancy. 3. A constancy is a sufficient condition of a change. 4. A constancy is a sufficient condition of another constancy.

For necessary conditions one can also distinguish four cases. But because of the interdefinability of the two main types of condition, every one of these four cases will be identical with one of the cases we distinguished for sufficient conditions. Hence we need not here pay separate attention to necessary conditions.

4

Our question now is: Are all the four cases which we distinguished possible instances of causal relations?

Let us take it for granted that a change can "cause," *i.e.* be a sufficient condition of, another change. This surely is the prototype case. It is interesting to note, however, that if this is the prototype case of a causal sufficient conditionship relation, then the prototype case of a causal necessary conditionship relation is that a constancy is required for another thing to remain constant. This is a noteworthy asymmetry in the relation of these two types of condition to changes (events).

An example should make this quite plain. Let us assume that the presence of oxygen in the environment is a causally necessary condition of a human body staying alive. Thus in the absence of oxygen no human body can stay alive (for more than a short time). But what does this last statement mean in "causal" terms, *i.e.* what causes what according to it? The answer is as follows: The statement amounts to saying that the disappearance (removal) of oxygen from the environment will cause, *i.e.* is a causally sufficient condition of, the extinction of life in a (living) human body which happens to be in this environment. It is thus a statement to the effect that a causal sufficient conditionship relation holds between two *changes*. And this is logically identical with the statement that a causal necessary conditionship relation holds between two *constancies, viz.* the (continued) presence of oxygen and the staying alive of a body.

Let us ask next whether a change can be a cause, *i.e.* a causally sufficient condition, of a constancy. For example: Could a change from $\sim p$ to p have caused q to stay on, continue present? The coming of p would then, as it were, have sustained q. This, as far as I can see, would count as a case of causal efficacy only if otherwise, *i.e.* if p had not come, q would actually have passed away. The coming of p "prevented" q from vanishing. But what does this mean?

It does *not* mean that the coming of p is a causally necessary condition for q to remain constant. For this, in the terminology of sufficient conditionship, is tantamount to saying that the continued absence of p is a causally sufficient condition of the vanishing of q. This would be a case of a constancy causing a change. Whether this is at all possible, we must also discuss. But this is not the case with which we are now concerned.

When we say that the coming of p "prevents" q from vanishing what is meant seems to be this: There is present, "in the background," a cause for the destruction of q. This cause, however, can be operative, *i.e.* actually effect the destruction of q, only provided that p does not happen or, as we could also put it, only under the circumstances $\sim p$. Assume, for the sake of argument, that this background cause with the power of destroying q is a change from $\sim r$ to r. The situation which we originally described by saying that the coming of p prevented the destruction of q was then, when more fully described, the following:

Two changes occurred, one from $\sim r$ to r and another from $\sim p$ to p, and a state q remained constant. These changes and constancies were so related that, if the change from $\sim p$ to p had not occurred, then the change from $\sim r$ to r would have caused a change from q to $\sim q$. The causal relation obtains here between two changes (in r and q), but is subject to the restrictive condition that the world should remain unchanged in a certain other aspect, *viz.* in the continued absence of p. If therefore there is a change in this third factor (p), when the first change (in r) occurs, then the second change (in q) fails to occur and there is instead a constancy (in q). The change in the third factor, as it were, "prevents" another change from happening and "produces" a constancy. A change with this effect is often spoken of as a *counteracting* or *intervening* cause. It is of interest to note that such a counteracting cause possesses no "causal efficacy" of its own—but is a cause only in the oblique sense of destroying the opportunity for the operation of another cause.

A concrete example may help us make these abstract lines of thought clearer. I walk up to the closed door in front of me and press my hand against it, thereby, as we say, "keeping the door closed." (It is assumed that the door opens inwards.) Placing my hand against the door obviously is causally efficacious in keeping the door closed, only provided there is some cause in operation which is such that it would effect the opening of the door were it not for the fact that something is pressing against the door, thus preventing the door from opening. Some other agent or force is, for example, pushing on the door from the other side, trying to open it. Therefore the change, which consists in my placing my hand against the door, is not a cause of the constancy, which consists in the door remaining closed. But the proviso that this change should not take place, *i.e.* that my hand should not be pressing against the door, is a requirement which must be satisfied (possibly along with a number of others), if a certain cause of another change, *viz.* the door opening, is to be efficacious. If this cause happens to be there, then my placing my hand against the door prevents the cause from being effective and thus acts as a *counteracting* cause.

We now turn the question the other way around and ask whether a constancy can cause a change. It seems that the answer to this question too is negative. The fact, say, that p is and remains absent cannot, by itself, cause q to vanish. But the absence of p may be required if a certain cause of the change from q to $\sim q$ is to be "operative." This means: the absence of p may be part of the frame within which this cause, say a change from $\sim r$ to r, effects the change from q to $\sim q$. If p had come, it would have acted as an intervening cause, preventing q from vanishing.

As seen, the case which we are now discussing is just the "mirror-image" of the case when a change is supposed to cause a constancy. In the one case there is a counteracting cause which prevents a cause from operating as it otherwise would do. In the other case there is no counteracting cause and the cause is allowed to operate. But the counteracting cause, so called, is no cause properly speaking; and in neither case is a constancy a cause or an effect.

It remains for us to consider the question whether a constancy can cause a constancy, say, p's continued absence cause q's continued absence. The thought off-hand seems implausible if by cause we mean, as we do here, a sufficient condition. (For necessary conditions this case, as was shown above, is the prototype case of a causal relation.) But here too we have to pay special attention to the oblique kind of causation which we call "counteracting."

To say that a constancy in $\sim p$ causes, $i.e.$ is a causally sufficient condition of, a constancy in $\sim q$ is tantamount to saying that a change from $\sim p$ to p is a causally necessary condition of a change from $\sim q$ to q. When would we assert either of these things? As far as I can see, we would assert them only if we thought that there existed but *one* way of effecting a change from $\sim q$ to q, *viz.* through a change from $\sim p$ to p. For, if there existed *other* ways beside this one, for example through a change in some factor r, then there would be no reason for holding the constancy of $\sim p$ "responsible" for the constancy of $\sim q$.

Let us therefore assume that the coming of p would cause the coming of q and furthermore that, *unless* this very cause is operating, q will not happen at all. The assumption is, in other words, that the change from $\sim p$ to p is a causally *necessary and sufficient* condition for the change from $\sim q$ to q.

Consider now a situation when p is absent and consequently, according to our assumptions, q is absent too. Normally, one would not—even granting our assumptions—think of this as a causal influence of the one constancy on the other. We would not say that p's continued absence "keeps" q absent too. But imagine a case when p is about to happen but is prevented—either by an interfering agent or by a counteracting cause. Then q too could be said to have been prevented from happening, and *this* relation between the two facts of prevention we should regard as a causal influence of the one fact upon the other. How is this case to be understood?

In this case too the causal relation is, primarily, between the two changes, from $\sim p$ to p and from $\sim q$ to q. The first of the two changes, however, can occur only provided a certain third change, *i.e.* the preventive interference, does *not* occur. The happening of the prevention is an instance of the putative case of a change causing a constancy. With this we have already dealt. We said that here the causal pattern is that of one change causing another, provided something remains constant which, in the case of prevention, happens to change (or is made to change) when the causing change takes place.

The new peculiarity of the case now under discussion is that we assume the causing change to be, not only sufficient but also necessary for the other change. That a change is necessary for another change, however, is equivalent with saying that a constancy is sufficient for another constancy. And this, we said above, looks like a case of causal influence only when the required change fails to occur because *it* is prevented from happening. Thus the change which is required for the occurrence of another change is a causally necessary condition for it only in the oblique sense that the negation of the first change, a constancy, is part of the frame within which alone the second change can ever occur.

5

The considerations which we have been conducting should make it plain that the question whether cause-effect relations hold primarily between events, *i.e.* changes, or between states, must be answered in favor of the first alternative. To say that a state *causes* another is, usually, only a shorthand for saying that the coming into being of the first causes the second to come. This fact must also be taken into account in a full and final formulation of (the logical skeleton of) causal laws.

But the discussion of the role which not-changes may play in causal contexts also revealed another thing which must be noted when we try to formulate causal laws in full. This is the fact that the efficacy of a cause on an individual occasion of its occurrence may be sub-

ject to the condition that certain features (states) of the
world remain constant on this occasion. I shall refer to
(the conjunction of) these features as the *frame* within
which the causal law holds good or the frame within
which the cause may become efficacious or operative.

When the cause occurs, but the conditions imposed
by the frame are not satisfied, the effect will normally
fail to materialize. That is: *that* cause will then not produce the effect in question. But there might have occurred on the same occasion another cause of the same
effect which is not dependent for its efficacy on the
same frame. This possibility shows that the constancies,
which are required in order that a cause be efficacious,
must not be confused with necessary conditions of the
effect. Not even in the extreme case, when there exists
but *one* generic change capable of producing the effect,
are the components of the frame necessary conditions of
the effect. They are necessary conditions only on the ad-
ditional assumption that the effect cannot occur *unless*
there is a cause producing it. This is an assumption of
determinism and, if made for all changes in nature, an
assumption of universal determinism. (See below IV, 3.)
The nature of deterministic assumptions I shall discuss
in the next lecture. Let it only be noted here that the existence and structure of causal relations (laws) are entirely independent of questions of determinism.

As far as I can see, it is not conceptually or logically
necessary that a causal law should be subject to the restrictions on its holding which a frame imposes. But it is
quite certain that normally a causal law is restricted to

some such frame. Is there *any* change, from $\sim p$ to p say, which is such that it will call forth another change, from $\sim q$ to q say, under *any* circumstances, *i.e.* quite independently of how the world in other respects happens to change or remain unchanged when p comes to be (and q is not already there)? An affirmative answer seems unlikely, though perhaps not *logically* excluded.

What belongs, and what does not belong, to the frame within which a causal law holds good is often left quite vague. Perhaps we know from experience that unless such and such factors remain stable the cause will not be efficacious. We also know that on any occasion when the cause instantiates hundreds of thousands of other changes will at the same time occur in the world, and also that hundreds of thousands of things will not change. The overwhelming majority of these changes and not-changes we consider completely irrelevant to the operative power of the cause in question. There will, however, usually exist a "zone" separating the certainly relevant from the obviously irrelevant events, and exactly where the border runs we leave—for the time being if not forever—indeterminate. This indeterminacy is given a familiar expression in a *ceteris paribus* clause. "Other things being equal, this cause will have that effect," we say. Here, "other things being equal" means that the world does not change in features which are relevant to the frame within which the causal law holds good. But exactly which these features are, we are usually not prepared to say.

This indeterminacy of the frame is important to the

testing of causal laws. Assume the cause is introduced experimentally in a situation when the requirements on its operation imposed by the frame appear to be satisfied. If the supposed effect nevertheless fails to materialize, what conclusion shall we draw? *One* possible conclusion is that two changes which for some reason we had come to think of as causally related simply are not thus related. Another possible conclusion is that we had not succeeded in articulating properly the frame within which the causal relation between the two changes holds good. Then we look out for further conditions to be included in the frame. It appears to be the case that the normal procedure is to let the failure of an experiment recoil back on the frame rather than on the (truth of the) causal law, once the latter has successfully stood just a few experimental tests. Whether this is so or not, the rejection of a causal law is not a mere matter of producing a negative instance—and the choice between *falsification* (of the law) and *correction* (of its frame) is in principle always present.

As already noted, the concept of the frame of a causal law is closely related to the concept of a *counteracting* (preventive) cause. A counteracting cause is a change in one of the factors which must remain constant if the law is to hold good in a given situation. The "effect" of the occurrence of a counteracting cause is that another change, which also happens, fails to produce the effect (a still further change) which, we think, it would have produced had the preventive cause not intervened.

Observations may suggest that something or other acts

as a counteracting cause on given occasions. But that this is really so is normally established by experimental interference with the frame within which, *ceteris paribus*, a causal law has already been experimentally established.

A counteracting cause is "oblique," or secondary, in the sense that its role is to prevent another, primary, cause from being efficacious. This primary cause we could perhaps call an *acting* cause.

6

Earlier (I, 10) we had given the symbolic expression $\wedge (p \to \vec{N}q)$ to the proposition that p is a causally sufficient condition of q, when q follows immediately after p. But it was also said that this was a first approximation only.

I have argued that the *primary* meaning of the statement that p is a causally sufficient condition of q is that the coming of p nomically implies the coming of q. How shall this be expressed in our symbolism? We consider here only the case when q is supposed to occur on the *next* occasion (immediately) after the occurrence of p.

A formula which satisfies the above meaning explanation would be this: $\wedge [\sim p \to \vec{N}(p \& \sim q \to \vec{N}q)]$. It can also be read: It was and will always be the case that if p was or would have been absent from the world on some occasion, then it was or would have been certain that either it is *not* the case that p is present and q absent on

83

the immediately succeeding occasion *or* it is certain that q is present on the occasion immediately after that one. If from this formulation we delete the phrase "or would have been," we get a sentence expressing the weaker proposition about *regular sequence* which is implied by a proposition about a *nomic connection*.

Speaking in the terms of our topological tree of possible world-histories, we can elucidate the above statement as follows: If a circle at any place in the tree contains the inscription "$\sim p$," then all circles connected with this one to its immediate right either will not contain the inscription "$p\&\sim q$" or will be such that all circles with which they are connected to *their* immediate right contain the inscription "q." An illustration to such a configuration would be this:

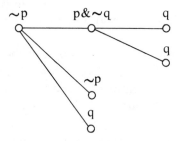

The symbolic formula given above can hardly be accepted as final, however. We must still qualify it so as to cut out certain "trivialities," *i.e.* cases which, if true, would entail the truth of the formula but which are such that we should not then wish to speak of the formula as expressing a "causal law."

One such case is, when the change from $\sim p$ to p is a

causal impossibility. This means that either $\sim p$ cannot obtain at all or, if it obtained, could never change. A second case is when the change from $\sim q$ to q is a causal necessity. This means that the state $\sim q$, if it came to obtain, could never remain for more than a moment but would instantly change to q. A third case, finally, is when there is no *opportunity* for the two changes to occur consecutively, *i.e.* when the compound state $p\&\sim q$ is a causal impossibility after $\sim p$. In all three cases, $\wedge[\sim p \to \vec{N}(p\&\sim q \to \vec{N}q)]$ would, trivially, hold good.

We can cut out the first and third triviality by adding to the proposed formula for the causal law the formula $\vee[\sim p\&\vec{M}(p\&\sim q)]$, and the second triviality by adding the formula $\vee(\sim q\&\vec{M}\sim q)$.

We shall speak of the added formulae as *contingency*- and *opportunity*-clauses.

By a (positive) *instance* of a causal law we shall understand a fragment of history which is an instantiation both of the cause and of the effect in their appropriate temporal relationship.[1] Thus, for example, the formula $q\&\vec{M}(p\&\sim q\&\vec{M}\sim p)$ is an instance of the causal law $\wedge[\sim p\to \vec{N}(p\&\sim q\to\vec{N}q)]$. The fragment of history $q\&\vec{M}\sim q$, which is entailed by the instance, we shall call its effect-component or -part, and the fragment $\vec{M}(p\&\vec{M}\sim p)$ we call its cause-component or -part.

Even though the statement that p causes q may be regarded as a convenient shorthand for the statement that the coming of p calls forth the coming of q, it does

[1] It is of some interest to observe that the notion of an instance of a causal law is most conveniently defined in accordance with the Nicod Criterion of confirmation.

not follow from this that the formula $\wedge\,(p \to \vec{N}q)$ could not, by itself, express a nomic necessity. But this would be a much stronger necessity than the one which consists in p causing q. For it would cover, in addition to the case when the coming of p is followed by the coming of q, also two other cases. The first is: when the coming of p is followed by the staying on of q, if q happens already to be there. That this is a nomic necessity entails that the absence of p is a *frame-condition* for the efficacy of any cause of the destruction of q. The second case covered by the more general formula is: when the remaining of p is followed by the remaining of q, if q is already there. This too entails that the absence of p is a frame-condition for any cause with the power of destroying q. The two cases thus jointly ensure that, as long as p is there, p will also *sustain q, i.e.* act as a preventive cause against any other factor which otherwise may destroy q. It is, moreover, not unnatural to think that if p is such that its coming has the power of producing q, then p will *also* be a sustaining cause, *i.e.* q will be certain not to vanish as long as p remains. But I do not think that it can be regarded, as part and parcel of what it *means* that p causes q, that p should have, in addition to its productive power, also this sustaining power.

7

Let us now compare the nomic statement $\wedge[\sim p \to \vec{N}(p \,\&\sim q \to \vec{N}q)]$ with the merely general statement

86

$\wedge[\sim p \rightarrow \vec{N}(p\,\&\,\sim q \rightarrow \vec{N}q)]$. The second says that whenever it is the case that p comes to be, it is also the case that q comes to be, provided there is an opportunity. The first says the same, but adds that also on those past occasions, when p did not come to be, q would have come to be had p come to be and had there existed an opportunity.

The universal validity of neither statement can be verified through observation or experiment. There is, moreover, no way of verifying the nomic character of the first statement even for a single occasion. But there is, I have argued, a characteristic test-procedure whereby we confirm the nomic as distinct from the merely general character of the statement. This procedure has two parts. (See above II, 3.) The one consists in interfering with events and producing a change from $\sim p$ to p, when otherwise it would not have occurred, and noting a subsequent change from $\sim q$ to q, if there was an opportunity for it to happen. The other consists in not-interfering and noting that, failing the first change, the second will normally not happen either.

In order that we shall be able to perform this *test of nomicity,* as I propose to call it, the following condition must be satisfied: It must be possible that there exist occasions on which (*i.*) p is absent and may either come to be or continue absent, and (*ii.*) both the presence and the absence of p on the next occasion is compossible with the absence of q. In our topological tree the possible existence of such situations would be exemplified by the occurrence in it of configurations like this one:

87

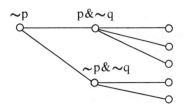

In our symbolic language again, the possible existence of such situations is expressed by the formula $\vee[\sim p\&\vec{M}(p\&\sim q)\&\vec{M}(\sim p\&\sim q)]$.

A successful performance of the "activist" part of the test for nomicity in a situation of the above description terminates—to use the language of the picture—in a circle in the upper bunch of the rightmost column in which "q" can be inscribed. A successful performance of the "passivist" part of the test terminates in a circle in the lower bunch in the rightmost column in which "$\sim q$" can be inscribed. A successful performance of the "activist" test thus results in a (positive) instance of the law.

The existence of situations which answer to the description we have given guarantees that the change from $\sim p$ to p is not causally impossible and that there are opportunities for the change from $\sim q$ to q to occur immediately after a situation when $\sim p$ obtains. In order also to guarantee that the change from $\sim q$ to q is not causally necessary, we shall have to rely on a successful performance of the "passivist" test. The very purpose of the "passivist" test can be said to be to guarantee that the

88

contingency- and opportunity-clauses of the law are fully satisfied.

The existence of situations of the above description, however, is only a necessary but is not yet a sufficient condition of the performability of either the "activist" or the "passivist" part of the test. This is so because the description, as given in the above symbolic formula and illustrated in the topological tree, says nothing about the interference or non-interference of an agent. It is logically possible that situations of this description exist, but that in no such situation can an agent *produce* the state p after the initial $\sim p$, nor *let* $\sim p$ continue absent. In order to give a full and final formulation of the test-condition of nomicity it is necessary to embellish our conceptual apparatus with one further distinction and with symbolic means for expressing it.

8

The "activist" component in the test of nomicity we have described as follows: We change $\sim p$ to p and observe q follow immediately. This description, however, omits an important thing from mention, or rather: takes it implicitly for granted. Assume that q too is manipulable, *i.e.* assume q is something we can produce when otherwise it would remain absent, and prevent from coming when otherwise it would originate. If the experiment is to show that it is p which is causally responsible for q, we must, of course, not interfere with q—neither produce it ourselves nor prevent it from coming—but *let* it come, as an effect of p's coming.

In order to express this condition of non-interference in a symbolism, we need a new symbol. This will be an index $_\phi$, to be attached to our "forward-looking" (see above I, 8) modal operators and quantifiers. That $\vec{M}_\phi p$ is true at a certain stage in the world's history shall mean that the state p perhaps obtains in the world at the next stage in its history, *provided no agent interferes with the world at that stage so as to produce or prevent p. $\vec{N}_\phi p$* shall mean that, on the same assumption of non-interference, p is certain to obtain in the world at the next stage. That $\vec{V}_\phi p$ is true of the world at a certain stage in its history means that, assuming non-interference, p may, sooner or later, appear in the world. That $\vec{\wedge}_\phi p$ is true means that, on the same assumption, p will be there in all future.

I shall say that $\vec{M}_\phi$ and $\vec{V}_\phi$ denote ideas of *physical* possibility—and $\vec{N}_\phi$ and $\vec{\wedge}_\phi$ ideas of physical necessity or certainty. These notions are a sub-species of what we called (I,8) *causal* possibility (necessity, certainty). One could say that the symbols with the index $_\phi$ signify that which is causally possible and necessary in a world from which agency is removed, or—as we could also express ourselves—when nature is "left to itself" (as far as the states involved in the description are concerned).

If something is possible in a world without agency, it is causally possible. But not necessarily *vice versa*. Perhaps this thing can occur only with the "help" of man.

90

Thus we have the relations $\vec{M}_\phi p \to \vec{M}p$ and $\vec{\bigvee}_\phi p \to \vec{\bigvee}p$. If again something is causally necessary, then it is necessary whether there are agents or not. But not *vice versa.* Perhaps this thing can be evaded or prevented thanks to human interference. Thus we have $\vec{N}p \to \vec{N}_\phi p$ and $\bigwedge p \to \bigwedge_\phi p$.

Now compare the two statements

$$\bigwedge [\sim p \to \vec{N}(p \& \sim q \to \vec{N}q)]$$

and

$$\bigwedge [\sim p \to \vec{N}(p \& \sim q \to \vec{N}_\phi q)].$$

The first says that it is a nomic necessity that any occasion when p is absent is sure to be succeeded by an occasion such that, if p is present but q absent on it, then certainly, *no matter what else happens,* q will be present on the next occasion. Here the phrase "no matter what else happens" is understood so as to cover also possible interference of agents with the situation under consideration. For this strong certainty we could use the name *inevitability.*

The second statement above is weaker. It says that, on the same antecedents as in the first statement, q will certainly, *provided no interference by any agent takes place,* be present on the last of the three successive occasions. This weaker certainty, subject to a clause of non-interference, is physical certainty.

We can thus distinguish between causal laws under which the effect of the cause is inevitable and such under which it is (only) physically certain. I think that laws which are established on the basis of experiments are typically of the second kind—and that it is normally a condition of the performance of the "activist" interference which is supposed to confirm the law-like character of an observed uniformity that, once the cause has been introduced, things should be allowed to develop without interference. Often we know, or think we may get to know, ways of interfering which would "disturb" the effect. Such interference is sometimes direct: we can suppress q in a situation when it is absent but would otherwise come to be. Sometimes, perhaps usually, interference is indirect: we can do something else, say produce a state r, which will prevent q from originating. But I doubt whether, on conceptual grounds, one could exclude the possibility of causal laws of the inevitability type.

It should be observed that the *first* occurrence of $\vec{N}$ in the above two statements of a causal law signifies certainty in the stronger sense of inevitability (causal necessity). That this should be so is indeed essential to the very idea of experimentally founded nomic ties in nature.

We can use the distinction between physical and causal possibility and necessity for expressing, for example, that the state p *can be* produced (through action) on a certain occasion. This is done as follows: $\sim p \& \vec{N}_\phi \sim p \& \vec{M}p$. The formula says that p *is not* there and that it is *physically certain* that it will remain absent but *causally possible* that it will come to be. The "residue" of possibility that is not "annihilated" by the physical certainty in question is the possibility that human action may make actual.

We can now also express such statements as that p can be produced on all or only on some occasions when it is absent, and that it can be produced on all or on some occasions when certain conditions are satisfied. For example: the formula $\wedge(p\&q\rightarrow\vec{N}_{\phi}p\&\vec{M}\sim p)$ says that *always*, when $p\&q$ obtains, we can destroy p. $\wedge[p\&q\rightarrow(\vec{N}_{\phi}p\rightarrow\vec{M}\sim p)]$ again says that always, when $p\&q$ obtains, we can destroy p, provided that otherwise p is certain to remain. The second is the weaker, and more "realistic," statement.

Finally, we can give a symbolic expression to the statement that p *is* there because it *was* produced—as distinct from being there through "natural change." This is done as follows: $p\&\vec{M}(\sim p\&\vec{N}_{\phi}\sim p)$. For, what the formula says is that p is now there but came to be after an occasion when it was not there and was, moreover, physically certain to remain absent.

9

We can now express in symbols a necessary *and* sufficient condition for the performability of the test of no-micity. This we do simply by adding a conjunct $\vec{N}_{\phi}\sim p$ (inside the outer brackets) to the expression given above in III, 7. We then get

(T) $\qquad \vee[\sim p\&\vec{M}(p\&\sim q)\&\vec{M}(\sim p\&\sim q)\&\vec{N}_{\phi}\sim p]$.

The possible existence of situations described by T means the following: It is causally possible that p is absent on some occasion and may either come to be or remain absent on the next; its presence and its absence on the next occasion is compossible with the absence of q; it is, however, physically certain that p will remain absent.

In the topological illustration we could mark the distinction between $\vec{M}$ and $\vec{M}_\phi$ by placing a sign $+$ inside the circles standing for world-states which can materialize only with the "help" of man, *i.e.* through action. A configuration satisfying the condition T could then be pictured as follows:

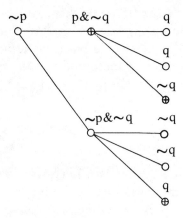

The figure shows a situation in which p is absent but can be produced. If p is produced and no further interference takes place, the state q is certain to follow. But

94

we could have prevented q. If again p is not produced, q is physically certain to remain absent, although by interfering we could also have produced it.

10

I shall conclude this lecture with a comment on a problem which puzzled Mill and which I myself find quite interesting. This is the question: why night is not the cause of day, nor day of night, although their succession is as perfect an example of a regular sequence as one could wish for. Mill saw in his question a counterexample to the "simple" regularity view of causation. The arguments by means of which he tried to show that regular ("invariable") sequence does not here amount to a causal relation are, however, confused and unconvincing.[2]

The day-night succession is out of reach of experimental test. But this, by itself, cannot be a reason why the succession is not causal. The reason must be in the *logic* of the case and not in factual possibilities and impossibilities.

Here it is important to note that day and night are related as the positive and the negative of the *same* generic phenomenon. If p is the state of daylight (at a certain place on the earth), then $\sim p$ is the state of night (in this locality). We can for our purposes ignore the inter-

[2] Mill, *Logic*, Bk. III, Ch. v, §6.

mediate states of twilight and also the fact that the occasions when day and night obtain vary in duration.

The crux of the matter seems to be this: No state can
be such that its coming into existence can cause *itself* to
pass out of existence. In order to see why this is so, let
us first consider the requirements which the world must
satisfy with regard to its possible developments, if we
are to say that the coming of a state p causes *another*
state q to vanish. What is required, in addition to the
non-existence of a case of $\sim p$ followed by an instance of
$p\&q$ followed by an instance of q, is the possible existence of alternative world-developments as illustrated
by the following figure:

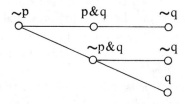

(Each total state after the first may have alternatives
which are not in the picture. But the alternatives should
be generically identical with the pictured ones in those
features which are indicated in the figure.)

Now assume that p and $\sim q$ were related as contradictories. Then, although it may, as a matter of fact, be
the case that there are no successions consisting of $\sim p$
followed by $p\&q$ (which now equals p alone) followed
by q (which now is the same as p), there could not possibly exist a world $\sim p\&q$ and therefore not possibly a

configuration of possible world-developments which would make it *logically possible* to test experimentally an assumed causal relation between the coming of p and its vanishing.

But could we not make ourselves the following different picture of the case when the coming of one state causes the disappearance of another:

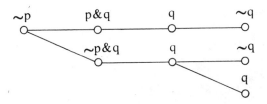

Here q does not vanish immediately but only *after* p has already appeared. (And we can think of the interval between the first appearance of p and the first occurrence of $\sim q$ as stretching over several occasions.)

If p and q are contradictories, however, we should be no better off than in the first case. We cannot *separate* the coming of p and the going out of q, because the going out of q means the going out of p, and *this* is the very change which the coming of p is supposed to explain. Speaking in the terms of Mill's example: We cannot imagine that day first ceased to be and night then came, because the ceasing of day *is* the coming of night.

Thus a discussion of Mill's puzzle, if I am not mistaken, supports the view that it is part and parcel of the *logic* of causal relationships that the configurations of alternative world-developments which constitute what I have called test-conditions of nomicity for observed regularities should be at least *logically* possible. Failing this, a uniformity of nature, however well established, cannot for conceptual reasons be a causal law.

Part IV

1

In this lecture I shall discuss the idea of determinism, and in particular that of Universal Determinism. These ideas have played, and continue to play, a great rôle in philosophic thinking. Some people seem anxious to take their truth for granted, perhaps "in the name of science." Others are equally anxious to oppose them, perhaps "in the name of freedom."

Our first task will be to discuss what the claim of Universal Determinism can possibly amount to. In its vague form the claim is that "everything has a cause" or that "nothing happens without a cause." These formulations challenge almost as many questions as they contain words. What does "everything" refer to? What is meant by "cause"? And what by something "having" a cause?

Let us dispose of the first question by saying that the answer to it can be gathered from the second of the above loose formulations of the deterministic principle. Then "everything" means "everything that happens," *i.e.* every event. This answer would be in line with what was said in the preceding lecture about the "dynamic" character of the causal relation.

By "cause" we shall understand a causally sufficient condition. If this conditionship relation is explicated in the way we have done it here, it follows that a causal relation subsists between logically independent, not conceptually connected factors. To include conceptual connections under the heading of determinism or determination would be neither unnatural nor philosophically uninteresting. I think that, in the realm of action and human relations, determination is partly a conceptual relationship. But for that very reason, it seems to me, is determination in nature also very different from determination in history and the life of societies. The grand idea of nature as subject to Universal Determinism is an idea of a nexus among logically independent phenomena. One of the philosophically interesting claims, associated with this idea, is that also the entire realm which the human and the social sciences study is part of "nature." It would be a trivialization of this claim to raise it in a way which makes it immaterial whether the phenomena for which the claim is made are conceptually independent or conceptually connected.

Consider two successive total states of the world. They will, normally, agree in some of their elementary components and differ in others. In other words: when the world passes from the one total state to the next, certain changes occur and certain states remain unchanged. What does the claim of Universal Determinism amount to here? Is it only that every one of the changes must have a cause? (This much is certainly claimed.) Or is it also that every not-change or constancy must be caused too?

Sometimes we expect things to change but find that

they do not. Then we look for, and often think we find, a cause which prevented the change. This observation shows that not-changes *can* be caused. But it would be premature to conclude from this that the claim of Universal Determinism must concern all not-changes as well as all changes.

Normally we are not interested in the question why things do not change. It is not part of our "ordinary," or even "scientific," curiosity about the causal mechanisms of the world why things do not always simply fall to pieces. Philosophers have sometimes wondered about this and attributed the cohesion of things to some "self-sustaining force" in them. But it seems wise to separate this idea from that of Universal Determinism.

We have argued (see above III, 4) that a cause which prevents a change from occurring must be a *counteracting* cause, *i.e.* a cause which operates against some operating cause of the prevented change. This idea, however, immediately challenges the question: what is the counteracting cause a cause *of?* It cannot, as such, be a (sufficient) cause of the not-change. For it has this effect only in the presence of another causal factor "working for" an opposite effect.

The correct thing to say here seems to be that the counteracting cause is no (independent) cause at all, but only a factor limiting the scope of another causal law. Thus the *one* causal law in this case would say that the change c_1 will under the circumstances C cause the change c_2 to take place. What prevented the change from taking place was the fact that a change in circumstances (*C*) occurred. This second change was not the cause of anything—but, if determinism is true, we may think that it was itself the effect of some further cause.

If this argument is acceptable, then the claim of Universal Determinism could be restricted to *changes* only. "Nothing happens without a cause" should then be taken to mean that no change occurs unless there is another change causing the first to take place.

2

Consider the following suggested formulation of the principle of Universal Determinism: Every change in the elementary states which compose the total state of the world at any given stage of its history has a cause, *i.e.* a causally sufficient condition which is a change in one or several (other) elementary states.

It is important to note that this one and a number of related formulations of the principle of determinism can be understood in two interestingly different ways. This fact reflects an ambiguity in the statement that a change *has* a cause (sufficient condition).

According to one way of understanding the above formulation of the principle it says that for every *generic* elementary change (among the states of the world) there exists at least one (other) elementary or compound generic change such that the second is a causally sufficient condition of the first. What this means is, essentially, that every kind of change is so related to another kind of change that, if a change of the second kind occurs, or would have occurred when in fact it did not, then a change of the first kind will thereby be caused, or would have been caused, to occur too. But the possibility is left open that a change of the first kind may occur without any cause at all.

This idea of determinism entails that any change which happens "in nature" could also be made to happen "artificially," if we learn to reproduce one of its sufficient conditions. If we think there are no intrinsic limitations to the learning capability of agents, we could also say that this form of determinism entails an idea about the unrestricted *simulability* of all natural events.

It is no decisive argument against this idea, that some changes occur in regions of the world which are inaccessible to human interference because of their remoteness in space or in time. The argument from distance (inaccessibility) would be valid only if some changes in inaccessible regions were qualitatively different from changes within human reach. Changes are "qualitatively different" when at least some different elementary states are involved in them. Thus, for example, the change from $\sim p$ to p is qualitatively different from the change from $\sim q$ to q—assuming that p and q are (generically) different elementary states.

I shall not here discuss the question when two elementary states should be considered generically identical and when they should be considered different. I have wished to bypass the question of what an elementary state *is* and whether there exist, in any "absolute" sense, elementary states. (See above I, 6.) These are questions of profound philosophic importance—and so is the question whether there are elementary states of affairs in other, to us inaccessible, regions of the world, which are different from those elementary states with which we are acquainted in our "terrestrial" experience. This problem is related to the question of whether the same laws of nature are valid throughout the universe. (See above II, 6.) I think there are conceptual as well as experiential reasons for a negative answer to the question of whether there are kinds of qualitative change with which we are not acquainted, and for an affirmative answer to the question of whether the laws of nature are the same throughout the universe.

I am not anxious to argue for the truth of the thesis that for every generic change which may occur in nature there exists some other generic change which is its causally sufficient condition. Still less I am inclined to defend a position according to which every generic change can actually be simulated thanks to human craft and skill. But I would wish to maintain that I cannot see any obvious objections on conceptual or logical grounds to the truth of these versions of the idea of Universal Determinism. I do not see, in other words, any intrinsic objections to the idea that anything nature produces could not also be reproduced (simulated) by man. I also find this idea of universal simulability philosophically interesting. But it is important that it should be discussed in its own right and not, as sometimes has happened, be confused with another, stronger, idea of Determinism.

The principle of universal simulability, if true, would also apply to all forms of behavior in living organisms, including men. But here a word of caution is in place. What are simulated are movements of bodies, *i.e.* natural events. We may or may not be entitled to speak of those movements as the actions of agents. But whether they are actions or not does not depend upon the accuracy of the simulation. It depends upon their place in a wider conceptual surrounding in which the notion of an agent already has application. The determination of this place is not a question of the existence of causal relationships alone.

3

The second way of understanding the idea that every change has a causally sufficient condition yields a stronger version of the principle of Universal Determinism. According to this second interpretation the idea in question means that no generic change can ever occur, unless it occurs as the effect-component of an instance of some causal law. (See above, III, 6.)

When a change occurs as the effect-component of a (true) causal law, we shall say that a cause of this change is *operative* and that the operation of the cause is responsible for or produces the effect.

The interpretation, now under discussion, of the deterministic principle thus says that whenever a change occurs it is produced by some of its sufficient conditions. Since this entails that the change, if it is to occur at all, must *have* at least one sufficient condition, it follows that the second interpretation of determinism is stronger than the first.

If a certain generic change is such that a sufficient condition of it is operative whenever it occurs, I shall say that this change is (generically) *determined*. The thesis of Universal Determinism, in its strong form, says that *every* generic change is (generically) determined.

That there *are* changes which are, in the sense defined, determined, we need not question. That is: we need not question that there are changes which, in order to happen at all, must be caused. The problematic proposition is that *all* changes are of this nature.

A change which is generically determined may, of course, have more than one sufficient condition. Sometimes when the change occurs it is produced by one, at other times by another of them. If on one and the same occasion more than one of its sufficient conditions are operative, we say that the occurrence of the change was on that occasion *overdetermined.*

To say that a certain change is determined is tantamount to saying that the *disjunction* of all the *sufficient* conditions of this change is a *necessary* condition for its occurrence. (Since one or another of the sufficient conditions must be operative if the change is to occur.) The disjunction of the sufficient conditions is, trivially, itself a sufficient condition. Hence the disjunction of the sufficient conditions of a determined change is itself a necessary *and* sufficient condition for its occurrence.

The disjunction of sufficient conditions can be transformed into a conjunction of necessary conditions. It follows from this and from the above that the strong thesis of Universal Determinism can be given two alternative formulations:

i. It is a necessary condition for the happening of any given change on a given occasion that *at least one* of its sufficient conditions should be operative.

ii. It is a sufficient condition for the occurrence of any given change on a given occasion that *all* its necessary conditions should be satisfied.

4

In the first and second lecture I referred to determinism as the view that world-history is linear. This means that there never were or will be in the ontic sense alternative developments ahead of us—though we in our ignorance may think otherwise. How is *this* idea of determinism related to the idea that nothing happens without a cause or, more precisely, to the idea that whenever a change takes place in the world it results from some or several other changes in accordance with a causal law?

The answer is that these ideas are *not* the same. Their relation is as follows: If nothing happens without a cause (the strong thesis of Universal Determinism), then world-development is linear. But world-development might be linear without causal laws reigning.

I shall first try to show that the reign of law entails linearity.

Consider two successive total states of the world, w_1

and w_2. Normally they will agree in some and differ in others of their elementary components. When they differ, a *change* has taken place. Assuming strong determinism, every such change is caused by some other change (or combination of changes)—and the common part of w_1 and w_2 may, or may not, be a required frame within which the cause has to operate.

Excluding the possibility that the causing change occurs after the caused change, we have to deal with two cases here: the case when the cause is another simultaneous change and the case when it is some change or changes in the past.

If simultaneous causation is possible, one could imagine that every difference between w_1 and w_2 is a consequence of *one* single difference between them. For this one difference one should then have to look for a cause in the past—in the first place in some difference between w_1 and the total state of the world immediately preceding it. The point of this observation is that one must step *beyond* the pair of total states w_1 and w_2 in order to get hold of *all* the changes responsible for the differences between those two states.

But what if the world has a beginning in time? Then there is a first pair of states beyond which, in time, one cannot step. Some differences between these first two states may have been caused by other differences between them. But at least one difference must be without a cause. There must exist at least one causally contingent event. It is this fact, maybe, which has made people conceive of a "prime mover" who, so to speak from outside the world, puts the world machinery in motion. The idea is philosophically far from uninteresting. It would be dispensable, however, if we allowed for an infinite supply of past stages of the world's history. Such a view of the infinitude of time is not unproblematic either. We shall here leave aside the problems which arise from the question whether the world has a definite beginning in time, a first total state. These problems are, after all, marginal to our main line of investigation.

If every difference between w_1 and w_2 is caused either by some other difference between these two world-states or by a difference in some earlier pairs of worlds, then there cannot exist any causal alternative to w_2, say w_3, which does *not* differ from w_1 in *all* the features in which w_2 differs from w_1. For if this were not so, then some of the changes which the world undergoes when it passes from the state w_1 to the state w_2 would not happen of (causal) necessity, but be only contingent. And this would be contrary to the assumption of determinism.

But could there not exist an alternative to w_2 which *differs* from w_1 in *some* feature in which w_2 does *not* differ from w_1? Let p be a state which is common to w_1 and w_2. The question is: Is it consistent with the assumption of determinism that there is an alternative to w_2, say w_3, which contains the state $\sim p$? We should remember that the presence of p in w_2 is not due to the operation of any cause—but that, on the contrary, p is there because no cause was operative which would have destroyed it. I find the question which was just raised puzzling. But I think the answer is that there cannot exist such an alternative w_3 (to w_2). My argument is as follows:

If w_3 is an alternative to w_2, it might have come true. Then there would have been a change from p to $\sim p$, when the world passed from the state w_1 to w_3. This change could not have been caused by any other difference between w_1 and w_3 which is also a difference between w_1 and w_2. Because then $\sim p$ would have occurred in w_2 too. It might have been caused, however, by some other difference between w_1 and w_3 which is not also a difference between w_1 and w_2. Then there must exist a cause for this other difference too, and so forth. Thus we shall ultimately be forced to go beyond the pair of successive stages on which w_1 and w_3 materialized and look for some change in the history of the world *anterior* to w_1 which is such a cause. This anterior change would then have produced the change from p in w_1 to $\sim p$ in w_3 with causal necessity, and w_2, which contains p, could not be an alternative to w_3. But the relation of being a causal alternative is symmetrical. Hence, if w_2 cannot be an alternative to w_3, then w_3 cannot be an alternative to w_2 either.

The above argument, if correct, establishes that the assumption of Universal Determinism entails that the history of the world is a linear flow of successive total states. In other words, this assumption entails that there are no causally possible alternative developments whatsoever in history. This, of course, is what determinism was always thought to imply (or maybe amount to). The question open to debate was whether the formulation which we gave to the deterministic thesis really implies this. I think it does. What creates a certain presumption for thinking that it does not is perhaps the following fact:

Whether something changes or not in the world depends, if determinism is true, upon whether there is a cause for the change or not. And whether there is or is not a cause for a given change on a given occasion is, in some sense, *contingent*. But in which sense contingent? Obviously in the *logical* sense, but not in the *causal* sense. For, under the reign of determinism, it is not only the case that effects follow with causal necessity from causes, but also the case that the causes themselves are the necessary effects of other causes.

5

Suppose the history of the world has a linear, alternativeless structure. Does it follow that causal laws reign too, determining all changes?

Consider a total state of the world w_1. That it is certain that it will be succeeded by w_2, that there is no alternative to this development, we symbolized by $w_1 \& \vec{N} w_2$. But this concept of certainty or necessity involves, by itself, no notion of generality or universality. It cannot guarantee, for example, that next time w_1 is repeated—if there is such an occasion—w_2 must follow again. Nor even does it guarantee that, if the entire history of the world from the beginning—if it has a beginning—and up to w_1 is repeated, w_2 must follow.

These are observations worth making. For it is an idea which philosophers have associated with the idea of determinism that, if the total state of the world is ever repeated once, then the whole history will be repeated again.

Our notion $\vec{N}$ might be called a notion of "step by step" necessity. The notion of necessity ($\wedge$) which entails universality ($\wedge$) is nomic necessity or "necessity under law."

The question is: Must we think of all non-logical necessity as being *grounded* in nomic necessity? That is: must we think that, if a total state of the world w is there without alternatives, then there exists a law which "makes" this state follow alternativelessly from past history—though perhaps not just from the one state immediately preceding it?

As far as I can see there is nothing which compels us to answer this question affirmatively. What I have called "step by step" necessity need not be grounded in nomic necessity. Some forms, at least, of such non-nomic (and non-logical) necessity are related to the notions of knowledge and certainty.

There exists in the history of thought a deterministic idea which is associated with non-nomic necessity. It is the idea that the course of world-history is determined, not by universal causal laws, but by the *foreknowledge* of a supreme being. This being, as it were, "sees" the world states follow one upon another in a linear succession. He knows what is going to be and his knowledge admits no alternatives which *may* also be.

I am not, needless to say, arguing here for the *truth* of such an idea of Universal Determinism. I am not even arguing for its logical possibility, *i.e.* self-consistency. But I think the idea is worth mention for at least two reasons.

It has, first of all, historical interest. It is a deterministic idea which was there before the idea of determinism under law became prominent. It is familiar from mediaeval Christian philosophy and associated with ideas of an omniscient and all-powerful God. In contrast, the modern idea of universal determinism was born under the impact of natural science and associated with the idea of the universal reign of natural law. It is a question of some interest whether ancient ideas of determinism, such as those which some of the philosophers of the Stoic school seem to have entertained, are more similar to the mediaeval-theological or to the modern-scientific idea of determinism.

Secondly, the idea seems to me to possess intrinsic logical and epistemological interest—quite independently of its truth or of belief in a divine being. It is interesting because of the light it sheds on the relation between possibility and knowledge. It is often said with emphasis that future events cannot be strictly known. Now assume somebody claims to know that p will be true tomorrow. If this claim is to be of any interest, p must be *logically* contingent. And the fact that p is logically contingent cannot, by itself, nullify the claim. (Perhaps p was true yesterday and we know this; still it may be logically contingent that p was true.) But can one make a self-consistent claim that one knows that p will be true tomorrow but also that $\sim p$ is possible for tomorrow? This question, I think, must be answered in the negative. One can conjecture that p will be the case, think this will probably happen, and yet admit as a possibility that things may, after all, turn out differently. But *knowledge* that p will be the case excludes alternatives. "I know that p, but perhaps $\sim p$" is a kind of contradiction, like Moore's Paradox. Therefore the idea of an omniscient being, who strictly knows everything that is going to be, is correlative to an idea of a world without alternatives. The alternatives which we, who are not omniscient, see in the world are only our "epistemic illusions."

The claims *we* sometimes, in fact quite often, make that we *know* what is going to happen are normally of a conditional form. We know that *if* this happens then that will happen too—for example that if I put my hand in the fire, it will hurt. This claim is at the same time a claim to know a causal law—normally on the basis of experiments and observations. In making the claim we may of course be mistaken. But what does "may" then mean? Surely we are not saying that it is *causally* possible that we are mistaken. This sort of possibility would make no sense here. What we mean is that it is *logically* possible that we are mistaken, *viz.* in our claim that a certain course of events is causally necessary, without alternatives.

If we know the causal laws, we know something

about the future. Can we *know* causal laws? I see no reason why this should not be *logically* possible. And therefore it is *not* true that we cannot know anything non-logical about the future. But any claim which we make to such knowledge may nevertheless be mistaken. That is: it is logically possible that things will be different in future from what we claim we know they will be. (And *if* they actually are different in future this shows that it is also causally possible for them to be different.)

Step-by-step determinism, if this means determinism to the exclusion of alternatives to the actual course of events, is determinism through *foreknowledge*. From this should be distinguished yet another deterministic idea, *viz.* the idea of determinism through God's "ordaining" things to happen as they do happen. God, it is then thought, steers the succession of total states of the world in conformity with his will. But if God's actions are at all like human actions, then this idea presupposes the existence of alternatives. "This *would* have been different, had it not been for God's hand," we could then say. This is a peculiar view of a divine being's relations to the world. But it should better not be called an idea of Universal Determinism at all.

6

If by Universal Determinism one understands the idea that the history of the world is ontically linear, then—as we have seen—one must distinguish at least two versions of the deterministic thesis. The one version is the idea of "determinism under law," the other the idea of "determinism through foreknowledge."

However, the idea of determinism under law also has several variants. The one which we have so far been considering is the idea that every change, when it occurs, is produced by another change in accordance with a causal law. This is a relatively weak version of determinism under law, a sort of "minimal version." We shall here mention and briefly discuss also a stronger version.

This is the idea of determinism which was given a well-known picturesque expression by Laplace in the beginning pages of his *Essai philosophique sur les probabilités*. A being with perfect knowledge of the total state of the world at some stage (moment) in its history and knowledge of all the laws of nature could with certainty predict what the state of the world will be on any future occasion and "retrodict" what it was on any past occasion. This fictitious being has become known as the Laplacean demon.[1]

Laplace himself seems to have thought of the idea as applying symmetrically to the future and to the past. But it should be observed that, unless we accept retroactive causation, the requirement of retrodictability is stronger than that of predictability. The future is determined, if everything that changes can be correlated with some other *anterior* (or at most simultaneous) change which is its sufficient condition. If the past too is determined, then it is required, in addition, that the suf-

[1] Laplace calls it simply "une intelligence."

116

ficient condition of any change is also a necessary condition of it. This requirement is not only stronger. It is also, I think, contrary to the experience which we have accumulated of the way causality "reigns" in nature. Therefore the retrodictive (retrospective) part of the Laplacean idea should better be laid aside as being of minor interest only.

We can, moreover, strip the formulation of its epistemic clothing, *i.e.* of the fiction of the demon or super-intelligence. For the "point" of the idea is not one about prediction and retrodiction at all, but about determination.[2] Given a total state of the world and the laws, all other posterior and anterior states are thereby uniquely determined.

This last formulation, however, does not seem entirely consonant with the "dynamic" view of causation as primarily a relation between changes. It may be doubted whether in fact it is consonant with any reasonable view of causation. How could knowledge of just *one* state and the set of all laws of nature be enough to enable the "demon" to practice his predictive skills, unless he also knew the "tendencies of change" inherent in that state: for example, not just what the temperatures are, but whether they are going up or down or are stable, not only the sizes of bodies, but whether they are expanding or shrinking or remaining constant, and so forth. What must be given is, so to speak, a total state

[2] Laplace does not speak of prediction and retrodiction but says, in his more pictorial language, of the fictitious intelligence that "rien ne serait incertain pour elle, et l'avenir comme le passé, serait présent à ses yeux."

and a "differential." Speaking in the terms of world-development through discrete stages: given must be a total state of the world and the fact that it agrees with and differs from the immediately preceding state in such and such features. Or, which comes to the same: given must be a pair of successive total states, w_1 and w_2. Or, speaking in the more sophisticated and specific terms of Laplacean world-mechanics: given must be the positions, the masses, and the velocities of the bodies composing the universe. And then it should be noted that velocity is not a "state" but a "differential."

In our atomistic and discrete model of the world and its history, the true equivalent of the "forwardlooking" half of the Laplacean idea is thus a thesis to the effect that, given a pair of successive world-states, w_1 and w_2, *and* the set of all causal laws, then all subsequent world-states are uniquely determined.

The question then arises: Is this version of universal determinism the same as the thesis which says that every change is uniquely determined by one or jointly by several antecedent (or simultaneous) changes? This is an interesting question and I am not certain about the answer. The answer, I think, hinges on the solution to a problem about causation which I have not discussed in these lectures at all. This is the problem of *contiguity* of cause and effect. (See above I, 10.) Can a cause operate "at a distance" ? (Here we are concerned only with distance in time.) If the answer to the question is affirmative, then it is *not* enough to know just one pair of successive states (and the laws) in order to be able to predict all future changes. For some of the changes which take place in the future may, in fact, be the effects of changes which were anterior to the given pair of successive states.

Laplace, it seems, assumed the contiguity of cause and effect. The present state of the world, he says, is the effect of the preceding state and the cause of the succeeding state.[3] But as far as I can see, there is nothing in what we have said here about the nature of causal laws and about the idea of universal determinism which would commit us to the assumption of contiguity. Nor have I been able to invent myself any argument for the position that contiguity between cause and effect should be regarded as a logical necessity, *i.e.* as something inherent in our concept of cause. But, since there is something both appealing and plausible about the idea of contiguity, I should not regard it as excluded that such an argument could be produced, relying at least in part upon premises to which I am already committed or should be willing to commit myself. But failing such an argument, the Laplacean demon version of determinism is *logically stronger* than the idea, as I have tried to explicate it here, that everything that happens has, when it happens, a cause.[4]

[3] "Nous devons donc envisager l'état présent de l'univers, comme l'effet de son état antérieur, et comme la cause de celui qui va suivre."

[4] Laplace seems to have thought that his deterministic idea was a logical consequence of "le principe évident, qu'une chose ne peut pas commencer d'être, sans une cause qui la produise." But the relation is, in fact, the converse of this.

7

I have argued that the distinction between accidental and nomic regularities is based on the idea of making experimental interferences with nature. It is essential to this idea of interference that there should exist alternative developments in the history of the world. But the idea of Universal Determinism denies this. Does it then follow that, if we accept determinism, we shall have to deny both the possibility of action and the correctness of the suggested way of distinguishing the accidental from the nomic?

Here we must be cautious with the answer. Perhaps we took a false view of the presuppositions of action and of the said distinction. What determinism excludes are alternatives *in nature, ontic* alternatives as we called them. But determinism does not exclude epistemic alternatives, *i.e.* alternatives which are, so to speak, relative to our ignorance. If the existence of such alternatives is all that is required for our concept of action, then we could reconcile the reign of determinism with the existence of agency and action and retain the idea that the nomic character of connections in nature is established on the basis of experiments, *i.e.* on the basis of findings which we obtain from acting in certain ways.

Is such a reconciliation possible? Can we remould our concept of action so as to become compatible with determinism? These are questions which remain for us to discuss.

Be it noted, however, that the possibility of reconciliation would be no proof whatsoever of the truth of determinism. We are always logically free to postulate the existence of a causal law which "ordains" that the total state of the world must be exactly what it is at any given stage of history. For particular states within a total state we often have a causal explanation at hand. And we know from experience that, when we have not got an explanation ready at hand, it may be worth looking for one. Perhaps, if we are patient and skilful enough, our search for causes will always be rewarded. But sometimes, or even often, it would seem much more sensible to *admit* alternatives than to *insist* on causes. The admission may give a new direction to research which is more fruitful than the search for causes. For example, we may become interested in finding which the alternatives are and how frequently they materialize, when an initial state is repeated. Interest in causes and deterministic developments would then be replaced by an interest in probabilistic developments. This change of attitude could be entirely satisfying to the scientist. But it would neither solve nor eliminate the philosopher's puzzlement about determinism. For the philosopher's interest is not so much in the *truth* of determinism as in its logical possibility. His interest concerns the self-consistency of a certain idea and, in particular, the reconcilability of this idea with ideas concerning action and human freedom.

8

The problem of reconciling determinism with free action can be put in the following form: Is it conceivable, *i.e.* logically possible, that every change or not-change which results from action has, whenever it occurs, a causally sufficient condition? The problem, at bottom, is whether the existence of such a condition is *compatible* with the possibility that the conditioned change or not-change is the result of an action.

It is one of the complications of this problem that one cannot discuss it thoroughly without bringing in the notion of time.

Actions normally take some time to perform. This is true even of simple actions such as the raising of an arm or opening of a door. It is questionable whether there are *any* instantaneous actions at all. I shall call the duration of (the performance of) an action the *span* of that action. And I shall here ignore variations in this span due to the fact that generically one and the same action is sometimes performed at a quicker, sometimes at a slower speed.

An action-span includes at least two distinguishable temporal occasions, answering to the initial state and the end-state of the action. For example: an occasion on which a certain window is open and another, succeeding one, on which it is closed. I have so far treated the second occasion as an *immediate* successor of the first (in a discrete time-medium). But this, in most cases, is an obvious oversimplification. For example: the arm which is being raised passes through a number of successive positions when it is neither in the initial position of hanging down nor in the upright end-state. To these successive positions answer successive occasions in time. Artificially at least, this temporal succession can be "chopped up" into discrete "bits."

There will thus normally be room also for changes *inside* the action-span. Not all of them need be related to the action. As my arm rises, other things go on—both inside my body and in the environment. Many of these things have nothing to do with the rising of the arm—for example, the ticking of a clock in an adjacent house. But others may very well "have something to do" with, *i.e.* be causally relevant to, the end-state of the action. Things which happen in the neural system of the agent as he raises his arm obviously have such relevance.

Now make the following experiment of thought: Assume that on some occasion within the span of an action there comes to obtain a state, say q, which is, under the circumstances, a causally sufficient condition of the coming into existence of the end-state, call it p, of the action. That this may be a true assumption seems undeniable. The problem for us is in the first place to see whether making this assumption would affect the description of the end-state as the result of an action.

It is essential to the description of something as an action that, when the initial state of the action obtains, the agent should be confident that the end-state p will not materialize, unless he acts. He may have this confidence even though the assumption we make about an "intervening" sufficient condition happens to be true—provided he does not anticipate its truth independently of his action. But does it not follow then that he is confident in something false? So that, in a sense, his thinking that he is acting is an "illusion" ?

That he is confident in something false would mean that he is mistaken in thinking that the end-state p would not have come about had he not acted. Now the assumption is that the end-state is the effect of an intervening sufficient condition q. Would it have come about had he not acted? Only if the answer to this question is affirmative does it follow that our confidence had been in something false.

Assume that the agent is totally ignorant of the occurrence of q. Then he cannot have intended to produce q on that occasion; it cannot be the $result$ of an action of his. Could it be the (causal) consequence of some action of his? If so, of which action? We are free to think that the only action that the agent performs in the situation under consideration is an action resulting in the end-state p at the last stage of the action-span. That the production of p could bring about q might seem very strange indeed. For it would mean that a state which comes to obtain later is a causally sufficient condition of an earlier state, or in other words that the effect would precede the cause. Is this possible? It is important, I think, to tackle this question with an entirely unprejudiced mind.

Let the hypothesis be that the state p on the ultimate occasion of a given action-span is a causally sufficient condition of the state q on some intermediate occasion within that span. How should we try to establish that this hypothesis is true? Obviously by means of experiments of the following kind:

There is an experimenter and an agent. The experimenter asks the agent to produce p. This is something the agent can do, provided there is an opportunity. The situation, moreover, must be such that the *experimenter* does not think that q will be there in any case, independently of the action of the agent. The agent obeys the order and the experimenter watches what goes on throughout the action-span. He observes q and p come about *in that order*. If these are the only changes he can observe, he would surely have a strong impression that they must be causally connected. But should he say that it is the coming into being of p which causes q to come?

Suppose the agent were to tell the experimenter: I can produce for your observation the state q. I do this by producing p. And he produces p, and the experimenter observes q a little before the action is completed. Must the experimenter then not say that what was *done* was the cause?

But what *was* it that was done here? If the agent does not himself observe or otherwise recognize q as anything resulting from his action, then we cannot attribute to him the action of doing q either. But suppose we can make him aware of q on the occasions when he does p—and aware of the fact that q comes first and then p.

Then we have taught him *a new action, viz.* the action of doing *q*. If these two actions are thoroughly familiar to him, he would hardly say that he does *q* by doing *p*, but put it the other way round and say that he does *p* by doing *q*. And he would almost certainly not wish to say that it is *p* which causes *q*.

If the experimenter, for some reason or other, wanted to have the state *q* produced, he might still order the agent to do *p*. But if the agent's answer to the question, how does he do *p*, now is that he does this *by doing q*, then the experimenter too would have no reason to think of *p* as causing *q*. The direction of causation would have been "restored" to the direction of time.

Let us go back to the situation as we originally imagined it and assume that the agent is ignorant of the occurrence of *q* and knows of no way of producing it. And let the hypothesis now be that *q* at the intermediate stage in the action-span is a sufficient condition of *p* at the ultimate stage. How would the experimenter establish that this hypothesis is true?

In order to establish this, the experimenter would have to produce *q* on an occasion when he feels reasonably sure that *q* will not come about unless he, the experimenter, produces it. Not only must he now not ask the agent to do *p*; he must either ask him expressly to refrain from this action (and then rely on the willingness of the agent not to cheat him), or he must look out for an occasion when the agent can be sure not to contemplate it. Assume now that, these conditions being satisfied, the experimenter produces *q* and sees *p* follow. Perhaps he repeats the experiment a few times. This might be enough to convince him of the truth of the hypothesis that the occurrence of q is, under the circumstances, a sufficient condition of the occurrence of p.

The agent, we assumed, is ignorant of the occurrence of q. But he may observe the occurrence of p. He knows, moreover, that p is something he can do. When the experiment is performed, he would say that p happens although he does not do it. If the occurrence of p is some change in the agent's body, for example that one of his arms goes up, he might feel some astonishment that this should happen. But, if the experiment is repeated, he would probably soon get used to this. Only if it happened so often that he could no longer on any occasion feel reasonably sure that it will not happen unless *he*, the agent, does it, would this influence his opinions of what he *can* do. Perhaps he says: "I used to be able to do p, but now I can no longer be sure, when I have set myself to doing it, whether p results from my action or from some independently operating cause."

Assume, however, that this does not happen, but that the agent retains confidence in his ability to do p, and that the experimenter has satisfied himself of the truth of the two hypotheses which we have been discussing. Then we should have all the assurance we could wish for that the occurrence of p is determined, *i.e.* has on all occasions an antecedent sufficient condition. This is so also when p occurs as the result of an agent's action.

I think the above assumptions are logically flawless and that they could be true for any action which we can imagine. Whether they *are* true is another matter. But the possibility of their truth should be enough to establish that action is compatible with rigid determinism in the sense that all *results* of action are causally determined.

The above conclusion must not be confused with the statement that all *actions* might be determined. What this would mean we have not even defined. Determination of action is not on a level, logically speaking, with the determination of states and changes. For this reason I should not wish to call it "causal" either. And I would separate an inquiry into the determination of action from an inquiry into causation and determinism in nature.

9

But now, would not the truth of the causal assumptions which we discussed in the preceding section entail that all action is an "illusion" only—in the sense namely that the agent thinks *he* brings about changes and states which would not otherwise be there, whereas in fact they would be there because of the operation of causes? Since we cannot be sure that the assumptions are not in fact true, must we not admit the possibility that we are constantly thus deluded?

These suggestions rest, I think, on a misunderstanding concerning what it is to be under an illusion.

Let us ask: Under which circumstances should we say that an agent *thinks* he is acting when, in fact, he is not? There are two cases to be distinguished. The first is when, upon the doing of something by an agent, there follows something else which the agent mistakenly thinks is a consequence, *i.e.* a thing causally connected with his action, although in fact it is not. Then he may also mistakenly come to think that he can do that other thing, *viz.* by doing the first thing. For example, that by raising his arm he can cause a big bang to occur in the room.

This is a genuine case of being deluded. I think we have all sometimes been in this way deluded as to what we can achieve by acting. We are freed from the illusion when we discover or when it is pointed out to us that the connection between the result of our original action and that other thing was only accidental. Another person may discover this and not disclose it to us—and then he can rightly say of us that we are under an illusion as to our abilities, that we think we do things which in fact come about independently of our action. But if nobody finds out anything of the sort, not even when the alleged connection is put to deliberate test, we consider the connection to be causal and the question of an illusion never arises.

The existence of causes for the results of our actions would not, of course, show that we are *in the above sense* deluded when we act.

The second sense in which an agent may be under an illusion as to what he does relates to his basic actions, *i.e.* to the actions which he performs "directly" and not by doing something else. These actions consist, normally at least, in moving parts of one's body—for example, crossing one's legs, lifting one's hand from the table on which it rests, or raising oneself from the chair in which one is sitting.

The kind of illusion with which we are now dealing is *not* the illusion which occurs when we think we move a part of our body, whereas in fact it does not move—say, because some muscles were cut and we do not realize this. The case with which we are concerned is when the movement takes place, as intended, but still cannot rightly be said to result from our action. Such cases are rare indeed, and many of us may never have experienced them. But they can be imagined and they sometimes occur.

Someone thinks he gets up from his chair. At the very same time some (to him invisible) agent, or perhaps the operating of a hidden mechanism, lifts him from the chair. Did *he* then not get up, *i.e.* must we say that he did not raise *himself?*

The answer would depend on the circumstances of the case. Assume the agent has been ill and for some time too weak to raise himself from the chair (in which one has seated him). He is getting better and makes efforts to raise himself. Suddenly he thinks he has succeeded—but, alas, he is mistaken: it was in fact the invisible agent who helped him to get up. We can tell him this and perhaps make him realize it by asking him to get up on an occasion when we know there is no-one to help him.

Assume, however, that the agent is in perfect health and has no reason to doubt that he can get up from the chair. He gets up, and when asked why he does this answers, e.g., that he is going to leave the room. If it is then pointed out to him that he was in fact lifted from the chair at that very moment—and thus would have been raised in any case—he could retort: "How strange that it should have happened at the very moment I rose." Neither he nor we would say that he was under an illusion, but would regard the operation of that peculiar cause of the result of his action as simply a coincidence.

But assume he could not give any satisfactory answer to the question of why he got up. "I just got up. But why? I don't know—perhaps there was something I ——, but I cannot remember." He is then told of the operating of the cause. Then he might say: "O, I see—I was mistaken when I thought I had got up myself, on my own." Here it would be wrong to say that the agent had acted, but since he was not very sure of or insistent upon this himself, we should probably not wish to say that he was deluded either.

Thus in the case of basic actions too, it is not the existence of a cause of the result of an action which shows that the agent is deluded in thinking that he acts. What would show that he is deluded is, for example, the existence of good reasons for holding that, although the re-

131

sult materialized, the agent is temporarily or permanently disabled from doing an action of the kind in question, or that he has not yet learnt to perform the action properly. The existence of a cause of the result is, in fact, *immaterial* to the characterization of the action as an "illusion."

But what if the "invisible" agent or cause were *always* there to help us do what we do? Would not the constant coincidence between the performance of the action and the operation of this hidden thing be very strange indeed? So strange that we should have to modify our view of an agent's freedom—even if it would not be right to label his acting "illusory" ?

To this should be said that the coincidence, as we now imagine it, would still be subject to some restrictions. Sometimes the cause operates when the agent does not act, and produces what would have been the result of his action had he acted. And sometimes the cause fails to operate when he sets himself to act, and therefore vitiates the accomplishment of his action. These are normal and familiar phenomena—to any one of us. If cases of the first kind were very frequent, we should feel unsure whether there is an opportunity for our action and thus unsure *when* we can perform it. And if there were very many cases of the second kind, we should doubt *whether* we master the action at all. So our idea of acting, of being able to do certain things, others not, depends upon the not too frequent occurrence and non-occurrence respectively of such discrepancies between causes and actions. That *this* requirement is sat-

isfied is a contingency. But it is nothing to be surprised
at. For, it is a condition which the world must satisfy if
we are to entertain our present notions of action and
agency.

10

I have argued that determinism is compatible with action *in the sense* that every change in the world which
results from the action of an agent, *i.e.* is imputed to
agency, might also have resulted from another change
which is its causally sufficient condition. This compati-
bility is subject to the condition that the agent has not
himself, prior to and independently of his action, antici-
pated the operation of the cause. This being so, does it
then not follow that action, though not an "illusion," is a
concept rooted in our ignorance of causes?

The idea that human freedom is relative to human ignorance is familiar from the history of thought. It is related to the idea, discussed earlier, of determinism
through the foreknowledge of an omniscient being. It
was given an aphoristic formulation in modern times by
Wittgenstein when he wrote in the *Tractatus* (5.1362):
"The freedom of the will consists in the fact that future
actions cannot be known now."

If action is correlative with ignorance of what is going
to be, is then not the openness of the future, which may
be said to be baked into our very concept of action, an
epistemic and not an ontic feature of the world-tree? On

this question, hinted at in the first lecture, I shall still have to take a stand before I finish.

Consider a total state of the world and its immediate development. Let us, for the time being, lay aside assumptions about linearity and Universal Determinism.

What is ontically certain about the world is that certain changes will occur, because there are causes of those changes operating. Ontically certain is also that some other changes will not occur, because there are counteracting causes preventing them. For the rest, the development of the world is ontically contingent, *i.e.* there are alternatives ahead of the given world. If determinism reigns, this "margin of contingency" shrinks to zero.

Similarly, there are two kinds of epistemic certainty about the world. One is the certainty *we* have that it will change in some features, because we think we know that causes of those changes are operating. The other is our certainty that the world will not change in some other features. This latter certainty may be grounded in knowledge of counteracting causes preventing the changes, but it may also be a "mere certainty" without any further ground. That which is not epistemically certain in either of these two senses is epistemically contingent.

Between the two kinds of certainty and contingency, the ontic and the epistemic, no logical relations hold. The ontic and the epistemic alternatives can be partly overlapping, or they can be inclusive or exclusive of one another. But any attempted description of the factual ontic alternatives would, of course, have to be in the terms of epistemic alternatives. For what we *think,* rightly or wrongly, that the ontic alternatives are, is reflected in the epistemic alternatives which we admit.

I have argued that if we want to establish, *i.e.* give our grounds for thinking, that something is ontically certain or is a causal necessity about changes in the world, then this presupposes an epistemic certainty regarding not-changes. This last is the certainty that some things, though not prevented from changing by any cause, will as a matter of fact not change unless *we* change them. The existence of this peculiar kind of epistemic certainty entails that we consider it an ontic contingency whether the world will or will not change in those features.

Now it may happen that this epistemic certainty becomes, as I shall say, "undermined"—and therewith also the entailed belief in an ontic contingency. This happens when the epistemic certainty is shown to have been "merely epistemic." The change *we* were certain would not happen would in fact have happened, because of the operation of a cause. That is: this change was ontically certain to occur. But the undermining of the original epistemic certainty and the establishing (as we think) of the new ontic certainty would again presuppose an epistemic certainty of the same kind as the undermined one. And this would entail belief in a new ontic contingency—and so forth for every further case of undermining the epistemic certainty.

Every time an epistemic certainty is undermined, the

135

margin of that which we consider to be ontically contingent will shrink. But the very process of undermining requires that there is some such margin left. And this means that only for *fragments* of the world *can* determinism ever become established. It is part of the logic of things here that the validity of the deterministic thesis for the *whole* world *must* remain an *open* question.

To say that to establish the ontic certainty of a change presupposes an epistemic certainty of the peculiar kind which we have described is but another way of saying that establishing causal bonds in nature presupposes action. It is by virtue of these relationships that I say that the *concept* of cause presupposes the *concept* of action. Action, however, cannot rightly be said to presuppose the existence of ontic alternatives in nature, *i.e.* the truth of some form of indeterminism. What action presupposes is only the epistemic certainty which, as long as it is not undermined, entails the belief in the ontic contingency of some changes and thus takes for granted a certain margin of indeterminism in the world.

Appendix

Some Modal Systems
and Their Tense-logical Interpretation

1

The four structures which we have termed "the logic of tomorrow," "the logic of yesterday," "the logic of the future," and "the logic of the past" are isomorphic with four systems of modal logic. (See above I, 8.) These modal logics are best exhibited in axiomatic form in two "stages." The first stage, which is common to all the axiomatized modal logics, consists of a set of axioms for "classical," two-valued propositional logic (PL) with the two rules of inference of Substitution and Detachment. To this common substructure is then added a superstructure of axioms for the modal notion of possibility (or alternatively for necessity). We denote possibility by "M" and introduce the notion of necessity by the definition "N" $=_{df}$ "$\sim M \sim$".

The following three axioms will then constitute a weakened version of the modal System M:

A1. $M(p \vee q) \leftrightarrow Mp \vee Mq$
A2. Mt
A3. $\sim M \sim t \qquad (=Nt)$

The letter t here represents an arbitrary tautology of PL, e.g. $p \lor \sim p$.

If to these axioms we add a fourth axiom

AR. $Mp \& Mq \to M(p \& q)$

we get an axiomatic for the modal System R.

If to A1–A3 we add

AC. $MMp \to Mp$

we obtain a weakened version of S4.

If we strengthen A2 to

A2'. $p \to Mp$

and then add

AD. $Mp \& Mq \longleftrightarrow M(p \& q) \lor M(p \& Mq) \lor M(q \& Mp)$

to A1, A2', and A3, we obtain S4.3.

For purposes of proof within the superstructure we must add to the inference rules of PL a Rule of Extensionality. It states that formulae which are provably equivalent in the modal system under consideration are intersubstitutable in formulae of that system *salva veritate*.

2

If in the weakened System M we replace M by $\vec{M}$ we get the tense-logic which we called "the logic of tomorrow." Here $\vec{M}$ should be read "perhaps (on the) next (occasion)."

If in the System R we interpret M through $\overleftrightarrow{M}$, we obtain the tense-logic of "yesterday," *i.e.* the logic of the notion "on the immediately preceding occasion."

If in the weakened S4 we replace M by $\overrightarrow{V}$, we get the tense-logic of the future. Here $\overrightarrow{V}$ means "perhaps on some future occasion."

If in S4.3 we interpret M through $\overleftarrow{V}$, we get the tense-logic of the past. Then $\overleftarrow{V}$ means "(now or) on some past occasion."

In linear time, the tense-logical interpretation of the System R is *also* the "logic of tomorrow," and the tense-logical interpretation of S4.3 is also the "logic of the future." [1]

---

[1] What is here called the System R was originally devised for capturing the logic of the connective "and next." (Cf. my paper " 'And Next' " in *Acta Philosophica Fennica 18*, 1965.) Krister Segerberg gave a more elegant axiomatization of the system and baptized it "the logic of tomorrow." (Cf. his paper "On the Logic of 'Tomorrow' " in *Theoria* 33, 1967.) If we accept that the future is "open" and the past "closed," the notion M in the System R must be given a "backward-looking" interpretation and the system itself renamed "the logic of yesterday."

Index

Index

Function (functional relationship), 3-4, 68-70
Future: logic of, 22-23, 137-39; openness of, 22, 26, 33-35

Generic (factor, state of affairs), 5-6, 11, 13, 62

Hegel, 14
History, 18-19
Hume, 53

Ignorance, 35, 133
Illusion, 124, 128-33
Implication: strict, 6, 9; universal (general), 6, 8, 10, 28-31
Independence (logical), 15-16, 55
Indeterminism, 19, 35, 136
Inevitability, 91
Instance (of causal law), 85
Interference, 39-40, 49, 51-53, 56, 63, 87-89, 94, 120

Knowledge, 114; *see also* Certainty and Foreknowledge

Laplace, 116, 119
Laplacean demon, 116-19
Law: of nature, 9, 60-61; reign of, 107-13, 120-21
Lawlikeness, 38
Linearity (of world-development), 25, 34-35, 107, 110-11; *see also* Determinism
Logical atomism, 15-16, 55

Manipulation, 57, 63-66; *see also* Experiment, Interference

Mill, 59, 95
Modal logic (modality), 22-25, 33, 137-139; *see also* Time

Nature, 58-61, 100-4
Necessity: causal, 9, 20-21, 27-31, 54, 91-92; logical, 9; nomic, 1-2, 9, 112; physical, 90-93; "step by step," 112, 115
Nicod Criterion (of confirmation), 85
Nomic, 9, 28-31, 36-39, 48-54, 83-87, 120; *see also* Law, Necessity, Regularity
Nomicity-test, 87-89, 93-95, 97-98

Occasion, 11, 13, 29, 55-56
Openness, *see* Future
Opportunity, 85

Past: closedness of, 24, 34-35; logic of, 24-25, 139
Possibility: causal, 20, 90-93; latent, 20; logical, 17, 95-98, 115; lost, 26, 34, 37; physical, 90-94
Possible world, *see* World
Power, 51
Preventive, *see* Action, Cause
Probability, 4, 61, 121
Process, 13-14
Productive, *see* Action, Cause

Quantifiers, 6-7

Regularity: accidental, 28, 31, 36, 49-52, 84, 120; nomic, 8-9, 28-31, 36-39, 48-50, 84-86, 120
Result, *see* Action